The Yukon and Northwest Territories

ANTHONY HOCKING

Publisher: John Rae

Managing Editor: Robin Brass

Manuscript Editor: Jocelyn Van Huyse

Production Supervisor: Lynda Rhodes

Graphics: Pirjo Selistemagi

Cover: Brian F. Reynolds

⊏⊐THE CANADA SERIES

McGRAW-HILL RYERSON LIMITED

Toronto Montreal New York St. Louis San Francisco
Auckland Bogotá Guatemala Hamburg Johannesburg
Lisbon London Madrid Mexico New Delhi Panama
Paris San Juan São Paulo Singapore Sydney Tokyo

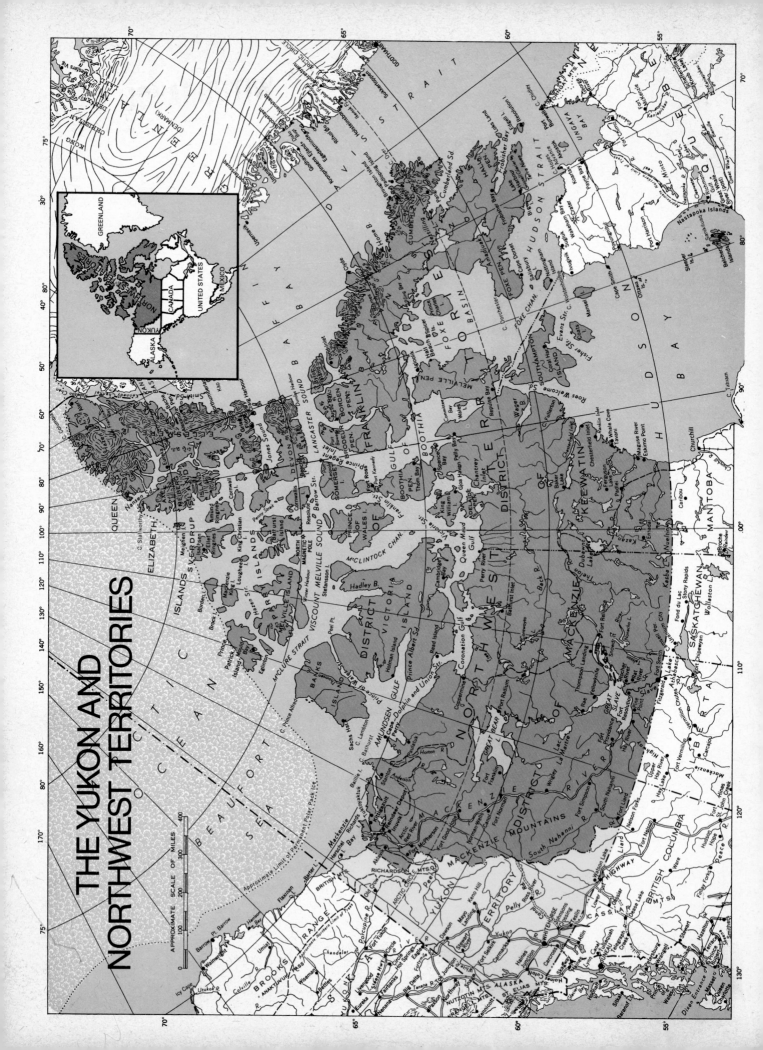

THE YUKON AND NORTHWEST TERRITORIES

APPROXIMATE SCALE OF MILES
100 200 300 400

CONTENTS

THE YUKON AND NORTHWEST TERRITORIES

Divided from each other by the Mackenzie mountains, the Yukon and Northwest Territories form a Canadian empire of the north. Taken together they occupy nearly 40 per cent of Canada's land area, even though they hold less than one-half of one per cent of the population.

The Yukon is world famous for its gold rush of the 1890s and the poems that Robert Service wrote about it. The 'Spell of the Yukon' that Service described still lures adventurers from all over North America, most of them searching for peace and fulfilment rather than the wealth that attracted the pioneers.

The Northwest Territories knew white men at least as early as the sixteenth century. Inuit have a charming name for the foreigners — *kabloona*, 'the ones with bushy eyebrows.' Since the 1950s kabloona influence has imposed itself on all regions of the N.W.T., developing its resources and forcing changes in its lifestyle.

The Yukon and Northwest Territories are still frontiers of the north, but they are also northern homelands. The N.W.T. is the one jurisdiction in Canada in which original peoples outnumber whites, by a margin of three to two. In the Yukon, Indians account for nearly one-quarter of the population.

The N.W.T.'s original peoples used to be known as Indians and Eskimos, but many dislike the terms. Instead they want to be known as 'the people' — Dene or Inuit, depending on their language. With some overlap in the Mackenzie river delta, Dene live south of the treeline and Inuit to the north.

In time, both the Yukon and N.W.T. will probably become provinces within Canada's Confederation. For now they are administered by territorial governments that are partially controlled by Ottawa. Their dilemma is to reconcile their frontiers with their homelands, and to allow all their peoples an adequate say in their futures.

Spring warmth creates magical effects as the arctic pack ice disintegrates and reveals the polar sea below.

THE YUKON

RIVERS AND MOUNTAINS

The Yukon's highest elevations are in the St. Elias mountains of the south-west, and the lowest are on the shores of the Beaufort sea. Between the extremes are hills, mountains, and great river valleys that provide some of the most glorious scenery in Canada.

The Yukon's hills and mountains are sections of the Cordillera, the complex of mountain belts that extends along the

Americas' western edge from Alaska to Chile. Geologists believe that the mountains were formed under extreme pressure when plates of the earth's crust interlocked or collided.

The St. Elias range contains some of the loftiest peaks in Canada, among them Mount Logan (6050 m), which is the highest of all. The mountains came into being partly through volcanic activity, partly through erosion that wore down surface outcroppings and exposed rock that was originally hidden deep within the earth.

The Mackenzie range of the east and the Richardson and British mountains of the north were formed by the folding and rupture of beds of sediment laid down at the bottom of ancient seas. In these cases, the mountains are much younger than the rocks that they contain.

The Yukon's interior is a plateau of rough, irregular upland that contains several minor mountain ranges like the Ogilvies, Pellys, and Dawsons. This is the area that contains most of the Yukon's mineral wealth — lead, zinc,

Kluane Lake, the Yukon's largest expanse of water. The lake is within Kluane National Park and is easily accessible from the Alaska highway.

Mount St. Elias, which gave its name to the surrounding mountain range. The mountain marks the Yukon's south-east corner, and it is part of Kluane National Park.

copper, asbestos, coal, and not least, several promising deposits of oil and natural gas.

The gold and silver that have made the Yukon famous can still be found in narrow veins of quartz, but most of the gold recovered by miners was in beds of gravel. Long since, wind, water, and frost eroded the gold from the rock that originally contained it, and it was washed away to be deposited elsewhere.

In most of Canada the effects of erosion were compounded by thick sheets of ice, the glaciers that flowed across the land at the expense of all that stood in their way. Much of the Yukon was affected too — there are still impressive glaciers in the St. Elias mountains — but large areas of the west escaped unscathed.

These unglaciated areas are in two sections, north from the Ogilvie mountains to the Beaufort sea, and south from Dawson to the St. Elias range. In both sections there are deep layers of soil and gravel, laid down on the river beds in the course of millions of years.

The rivers have cut deeply into the Yukon's mountains and the interior plateau too. In places their valleys are broad and flat-bottomed, in others narrow and sheer. Most of the rivers rise in the Cordillera and flow north or westwards with the slope of the land.

That is the case with the Pelly, Stewart, and Porcupine rivers, once important as fur-trading routes. The Klondike river, famous for its gold rush, follows the same pattern. All are tributaries of the Yukon, an Indian name meaning 'great river.' The Yukon rises barely 30 km from the Pacific yet travels more than 3000 km before it reaches the ocean in the Bering strait.

The east-central Yukon, however, is drained by rivers that flow into the Mackenzie river system, leading to the polar sea. So is the south-east, emptied by the Liard. Rivers of the far north travel direct to the Beaufort sea.

The Porcupine caribou herd roams the barrens between Old Crow and the sea. The herd winters in the Yukon and in spring moves towards calving grounds in Alaska.

The Vegetation

The high barrier of the St. Elias mountains intercepts moist air from the Pacific, and most of the Yukon receives only limited precipitation. If temperatures were not so low, much of the territory would be considered a desert.

Pacific air does help to moderate the low temperatures, and is forever locked in combat with cold air sweeping southwards from the arctic. As a result the Yukon experiences constantly fluctuating temperatures both in winter and summer, and even in the north mid-summer temperatures can be surprisingly warm.

The frost-free growing season is necessarily short, but it is balanced by almost continuous sunlight during June, July, and August. Agriculture suffers more from lack of precipitation than from frost. Trees, however, take

hold and grow. Dense forests cover the south-east and thin only gradually towards the west and north, and the treeline extends north of the arctic circle.

White spruce dominate most of the Yukon's forest areas, together with

lodgepole pines, aspens, larches, alpine firs, and black spruce. In the north, stunted black spruce stand out against the shrubs and tussock that have taken root where soil has been formed, and against the lichens that colonize the barren rock.

Miles Canyon on the Yukon river at Whitehorse, once a sequence of rapids but now tamed by a hydro dam downstream.

Public Archives Canada C-2263

Kutchin hunters in 1820, as drawn by the missionary A. H. Murray. Early contact with Russian traders in Alaska provided the Kutchin with firearms to pursue furbearers and fight their enemies.

Kutchin of the northern Yukon take part in a drum dance, about 1820. Their descendants still live in the Old Crow region today. Another drawing by A. H. Murray.

Public Archives Canada C-2169

The Bone Age

Parts of the Yukon and Alaska escaped the glaciers, and archaeologists believe that they served as refuges both for hunters and for the animals they hunted. Sites have been located that were occupied by man 30 000 years ago and perhaps even earlier.

The region of Old Crow in the northern Yukon has produced human remains dating from 20 000 years ago, but even more significant are large quantities of animal bones that were evidently used as tools. Their contemporaries elsewhere shaped stones, but early Yukoners apparently recycled the remains of mammoths, bison, and caribou to make cutting edges and scrapers.

Archaeologists suggest that the hunters reached North America by means of a land bridge across what is now the Bering strait. At peaks of glacial activity so much water was tied up in the ice sheets that large areas of the seabed were exposed. That has happened in at least three periods during the last 70 000 years.

Not only the hunters but also their prey would have taken refuge in areas where ice and frost had not removed the vegetation. As corridors opened in the ice, the hunters moved southwards and other peoples followed them across the Bering region — the ancestors of Canada's Indians and of the Inuit.

There were Inuit living on Herschel Island off the Yukon's coast until quite recent times, many of them involved in helping the American whalers who visited the region each year. With the collapse of the whaling industry, the families went to the Mackenzie delta, and there are no more Inuit living in the Yukon.

The Indians of the Yukon fall into two main groups speaking separate languages. South of Whitehorse are the Tagish, Tlingit-speakers related to tribes of the coast. For centuries the Tagish have had close trading links with bands of the interior, but have also lived by fishing and trapping in the forest.

Otherwise the Yukon's bands are Athapaskan-speaking. Those in the drainage basin in the upper Yukon are Loucheux ('squint-eyes,' referring to their oriental features). They too have been people of the forest. Farther north are the Kutchin of the Old Crow region, people of the caribou and of the muskrat that abound on the Old Crow flats.

EARLY VISITORS

Public Archives of Canada C-2157

Capt. John Franklin and his men on their way to Herschel Island in 1829. A water-colour by Lt. George Back.

In 1741 the Danish navigator Vitus Bering approached the Alaskan coast and claimed it for Russia. In the distance he sighted a high peak that he named Mount St. Elias. Today the mountain marks the Yukon's south-western corner.

Bering's discoveries led Russian fur traders to Alaska, and trade goods like metal arrow-tips reached Indians and Inuit far to the north and east. The unfriendly rivalry between Russian traders and competitors from Eastern Canada led Russia and Britain to negotiate a boundary between their spheres of influence.

The two countries reached agreement in 1825. By coincidence, that was the year when the first white visitor set foot in what is now the Yukon. He was the British explorer John (soon to be Sir John) Franklin, sent overland by the British government to search for a sea passage to the Pacific.

Franklin had travelled from New York by way of the Great Lakes and the northern prairies, then down the Mackenzie river. At the mouth he turned west, intending to meet another British expedition. It was supposed to be sailing eastwards from the Pacific along Alaska's northern coast and would carry him home to Britain.

So it was that Franklin and his party arrived at Herschel Island, the only one in the Yukon. The explorer named it to honour the astronomer William Herschel. He discovered the island was inhabited by some 50 Inuit who possessed metal arrows traded from white men to the west, presumably Russians.

Franklin proceeded westwards, but could not locate the other expedition. He returned to the Mackenzie and so to the south, on the way noting large numbers of caribou and other furbearers. His reports prompted the Hudson's Bay Company to send an expedition of its own to evaluate the whole area for trade.

The Hudson's Bay expedition was led by John Bell, who in 1840 founded Fort McPherson on the Mackenzie delta. In the years that followed, Bell travelled extensively, exploring the Porcupine river and reaching its junction with the majestic Yukon river in what is now Alaska.

At the junction Bell established Fort Yukon, and in 1847 he built an outpost, Lapierre House, east of the present site of Old Crow. Meanwhile, another Hudson's Bay representative was in the south of the territory. Robert Campbell had been sent to explore the upper Liard river and the land to the west.

In 1842, Campbell had built a small post on the Pelly river, and in the next year he travelled downstream until he met the Yukon. There in 1844 he built Fort Selkirk, which quickly attracted Indians who had previously traded their furs to coastal tribes. For years, those tribes had been acting as middlemen for the Russians.

The new post thrived until 1852. Then when Campbell and many of his men were away, coastal Indians swooped on the fort and massacred most of those who remained. The marauders escaped with their plunder, and Campbell sent the survivors downstream to Fort Yukon. He asked for permission to re-establish his post but was refused.

Fort Selkirk was gone, but the company had other outposts. Their operations were so successful that the Russians were losing more in Alaska than they were gaining. Perhaps in revenge, in 1867 the Russians sold the whole territory to the United States at a bargain price, and the Yukon had a new neighbour.

The Yukon river, which rises barely 30 km from the Pacific, yet travels more than 3000 km before it reaches the ocean in the Bering strait.

KLONDIKE FEVER

The 1860s saw an impressive gold rush to the Cariboo in British Columbia, which attracted fortune-hunters from all over North America. They also saw the first reported discovery of gold in the Yukon, by a young Anglican missionary named Robert McDonald.

The discovery seemed unimportant compared with finds to the south. Even so, prospectors were ranging farther north as the Cariboo fields faced exhaustion. During the 1880s there were modest discoveries on two tributaries of the Yukon river, the Stewart and the Fortymile, and mining began in earnest.

That was the situation in August 1896 when an American frontiersman and his four companions arrived on Rabbit Creek, an unimpressive tributary of the Klondike river. The American was George Carmack, and his companions were his Indian wife Kate, her brother 'Skookum Jim' Mason, and 'Tagish Charley.'

Carmack was not a prospector and made a living through fishing and cutting wood. He had recently been invited to join miners working claims in another valley, but spurned the offer because his Indians were not wanted. Skookum Jim had been urging him to take up prospecting, but he insisted that he had no interest in it.

Quite what happened on Rabbit Creek is not clear, but it seems that Skookum Jim panned gravel in the stream. To his excitement he could see gold dust between the pebbles 'like cheese in a sandwich.' Quickly the men staked four claims — two for Carmack, one each for the Indians — and raced to Fortymile to register them.

Rabbit Creek was immediately renamed Bonanza, many times richer than the deposits already being worked. Fortymile was virtually abandoned as miners packed their belongings and rushed to the Klondike. Within a month more than 200 claims were staked, and miners scrambled to dig through to bedrock in search of dust and nuggets.

Winter arrived, and the Klondike was isolated from the outside world for five months. By early summer many fortunes were made, and miners with gold in their pockets travelled to the coast to take ship for the south. One party travelled to Seattle on board the *Portland,* another to San Francisco on the *Excelsior.*

The ships' arrival caused a sensation. It was said they carried 'a ton of gold' apiece — most of it in the baggage of miners who meant to sell it to American mints. At the time, the United States was going through a depression, and the ships' return passages to Alaska were immediately booked solid.

So began the Klondike stampede. The promise of gold attracted fortune-hunters from many countries, but most of those in the initial rush were from the western United States. Scores more ships were pressed into service, heavily laden with would-be prospectors and their equipment bound for the north.

There were several routes to the goldfields. The easiest was also the longest — by sea to the Bering strait, then up the Yukon to the Klondike's mouth. The trip could be made only during summer when the river was not frozen, but later became a popular route for supply vessels.

Some prospectors reached the Klondike overland, starting in northern British Columbia or in a few cases from Edmonton in Alberta. However, most sailed to Skagway or Dyea on the coast of the Alaska panhandle, aiming to climb over the St. Elias mountains on foot and then reach the Klondike by the Yukon river.

The trail from Skagway was known as the White Pass route, supposed to be fit for packhorses. Too late, stampeders discovered the trail was a hazardous mountain path strewn with huge rocks.

Miners use 'rockers' to wash gold-bearing muck mined from a dried-up streambed in the Klondike region.

National Photography Collection C-399

One section of the trail is still known as 'Dead Horse Gulch' in memory of thousands of casualties.

Worse, the White Pass route was infested by confidence men working for the notorious 'Soapy' Smith of Skagway. The gang fleeced both greenhorns ('cheechakos') and veterans ('sourdoughs') until in 1898 Smith was killed in a Skagway gunfight and his men were run out of town.

The route from Dyea was known as the Chilkoot trail, free of gangsters but involving a steep climb to the pass that led into Canadian territory. Both there and in the White Pass, Canadian mounted police allowed nobody through unless they were equipped with enough supplies to last them a year.

Chilkoot climbers usually had to make many trips to ferry their baggage to the top and down the other side. A man took his place in the long line trudging up the slope at an angle of 35°, and hardly dared to step aside in case he was not allowed back. He cached his possessions at the top, then slid down to fetch another load.

Dog teams provided efficient transport links between the far-flung corners of the Klondike goldfields. In the background is a row of windlasses topping claims that followed the line of Bonanza Creek.

The two trails converged on Bennett Lake in northern British Columbia. There stampeders cut down trees and whipsawed timber to build boats. With the spring thaw of 1898, more than 2000 small craft set off on a hazardous journey of more than 800 km. As summer advanced, the Klondike's population swelled to tens of thousands.

The Mines

Even at Fortymile miners found that the richest deposits of gold lay close to the bedrock, deposited there by ancient streams. To reach it they had to excavate a shaft through frozen mud and gravel, then tunnel a 'drift' that followed the paydirt.

This was the technique used on the Klondike fields too, but in both locations there was a complication. The ground was frozen, at least during the winter, and before any could be removed it had to be thawed. Miners lit wood fires to defrost a few centimetres of 'muck,' shovelled it out, then began again.

As the shaft deepened the miners used buckets to haul muck to the surface. Gold-bearing gravels from near the bedrock were piled separately from the useless dirt. In the spring the miners washed them in sluiceboxes that trapped gold particles while allowing the remainder to flow away.

As the gold rush progressed, claimholders improved their methods. Many introduced a steam boiler, piping steam to the frozen working face to produce a continuing thaw. Others set up a self-dumping windlass on top of the shaft, to carry buckets of gravel direct to the sluice boxes.

National Photography Collection C-5395
Reaching bedrock, Yukon miners followed gold-bearing gravel along the course of ancient streambeds to the limits of their claims.

Dawson's location was superb, but in its early days it consisted of makeshift log shanties fronting on to untidy streets, and tents on the higher ground behind. Nearly every cabin was a place of business with a gaudy sign outside — laundry, tailor's, saloon, dentist's, cigar store, barber's, and even dressmaker's.

Especially in summer when daylight was continuous, Dawson was filled with activity. New cheechakos prepared to leave for the creeks, and veteran sourdoughs — named for the yeast substitute they used to make bread — arrived in town with their 'pokes' or moneybags full of gold dust. Stores and saloons were perpetually open — except on Sundays, when they were obliged to close.

Gold dust was currency in Dawson, and portable scales were standard equipment. There were confidence crimes galore, but surprisingly little violence. A strong force of mounted police made sure that no guns were carried, and deterred mischief-makers before they could do harm.

As the population prospered, there were demands for better goods and services and more efficient transportation. More steamers sailed direct to Dawson City by way of the Bering strait. Aerial tramways helped those who ascended the Chilkoot trail, and shallow-draft sternwheelers from British Columbia were introduced to the Yukon's upper reaches.

Most ambitious of all, a company was formed to drive a railroad through the White Pass route. Trellis bridges had to be built, and rock ledges had to be blasted from the faces of mountains. In 1900 construction crews that had started from the south and north met at Carcross, where the railroad's last spike was driven home.

The White Pass and Yukon route quickly absorbed all traffic crossing the mountains. Travellers were carried from Skagway to Whitehorse, the site of dangerous rapids that had caused many

DAWSON CITY

The stampede that had begun in 1897 showed no sign of dying, and thousands more fortune-hunters descended on the Klondike. Many of the later arrivals had no interest in staking a claim, but had every hope of making money from those who were already established.

By this time claims were being worked across 150 km of territory — not creeks alone, but also ancient streambeds that had dried up long ago. This whole area depended on a single boomtown that had sprung up where the Klondike river met the Yukon — Dawson City, named after a government geologist.

Gold dredges like this one were in use until the 1960s, scooping low-grade muck from flooded claims and washing out the gold it contained.

Mounted Police

Even before the Klondike stampede, a force of mounted police was sent to keep the peace at the Fortymile mining camp. Besides, the Canadian government wanted to make it clear that the Yukon goldfields were in Canadian territory and not in Alaska.

So it was that the police were on hand to meet the stampeders of 1897 and 1898. In command were James Walsh, the Yukon's first commissioner, and Superintendent Sam Steele. Soon the force's headquarters were moved to Dawson, and its strength was much increased. Besides, the Canadian government sent 200 men from the permanent militia — the Yukon Field Force — to guard prisoners, banks, and gold shipments.

After the turn of the century it was rumoured that a secret society in Alaska planned an armed invasion of the Yukon. The mounted police were kept up to strength even though the population was declining. Nothing happened, and in 1903 Canada and the United States made a final decision on their common boundary.

In 1904 the police began their

National Photography Collection PA 17031

The Dawson City detachment of the North West Mounted Police fires a salute in 1901. The force was becoming strong enough to keep the peace and save the Yukon from the rule of the gun.

famous patrols of outlying areas, carrying mail and visiting Indians and isolated trappers and prospectors. Winter and summer, patrols travelled from Dawson to Fortymile, Selkirk, Mayo, and Minto. There were also special patrols to Fort McPherson on the Mackenzie delta, a trip of nearly 800 km.

There were few mishaps on these patrols, but in the winter of 1911 four men with dog teams lost their way between Fort McPherson and Dawson. For days they sought a pass through the Ogilvie mountains, less than 50 km from their goal. Faced with starvation they turned back, but all perished within a short distance of Fort McPherson. Their frozen bodies were found by another patrol sent out to look for them.

deaths. There they transferred to a sternwheeler, and covered the remaining distance to Dawson in comparative luxury.

Dawson's wealth brought it respectability. As more permanent premises were erected, the mounted police herded Dawson's more seedy elements across the river to Klondike City, better known as Lousetown. Many saloonkeepers followed them, as the main town became more fitted for the middle-class families that were settling there.

By the early years of the century Dawson's boom was over. The most accessible gold was exhausted, and many stampeders had already departed with their fortunes made or their dreams shattered. Mining entrepreneurs combined blocks of claims to extract lower-grade gravels.

Shafts were no longer practical, and instead the new companies introduced heavy equipment. Horse-drawn scrapers and steam shovels stripped muck from the surface and scooped out the gravel beneath. From 1905, dredges the size of houses were built to feed sluiceboxes for 24 hours of the day.

Dawson City's main street in the summer of 1899. Both British and American flags are flying, and banners advertising dentists, sternwheelers, a shaving parlour, and many other interests are strung across the thoroughfare.

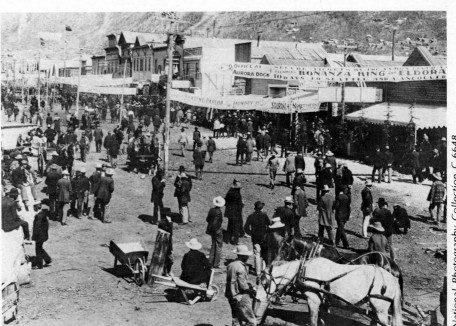

National Photography Collection PA 13320

THE RIVERBOATS

Three sternwheelers have been restored for tourists and sit high and dry on the Yukon riverbank. Others have been converted into holiday cottages, or have been abandoned to rot in the woods. The hulks are all that remain of many scores of paddle-steamers that once plied the Yukon's waterways.

Two small riverboats sailed the Yukon even before the rush to the Klondike, travelling from St. Michael at the mouth as far as the Fortymile miners' camp. The stampede proper attracted steamboats from as far away as British Columbia and the north-western United States, and nearly 60 of them arrived in Dawson in 1898.

Some of the boats were too cumber-

In Dawson City, passengers crowd aboard the last steamer of the season as it prepares to sail for Whitehorse, c. 1900.

Alaska Highway

Japan entered World War II late in 1941 and seemed poised to occupy Alaska's Aleutian islands. Alaska's mainland was threatened too, and the United States requested Canada's permission to build a military road providing safe access from the south.

Several routes were considered, and the one selected was farthest inland, well away from the risk of enemy attack. It began at Dawson Creek in northern British Columbia, crossed the 60th parallel near Watson Lake, and proceeded towards Fairbanks by way of Whitehorse and Kluane Lake. The total distance was 2437 km.

Even before construction crews began work on the Canadian sections of the highway, airports were built at Whitehorse and Watson Lake. Then 10 000 American troops and 5000 civilians arrived to push through the road, equipped with whole fleets of bulldozers and trucks and working from both ends to meet in the middle.

In many places there were muskeg and permafrost, which when disturbed left the ground a swampy morass. The construction crews piled up brushwood two metres deep and laid a gravel surface on top of it, or made wide detours to take advantage of solid rock. Streams were bridged, mosquitoes were braved, and the completed highway was opened in November 1942.

The Alaska highway remains in service today, but another wartime project is all but forgotten. There was a remote oilfield at Norman Wells on the Mackenzie river. The United States was given permission to build a refinery at Whitehorse and a pipeline to link it with the oilfield, more than 800 km away, as well as links with Skagway and Fairbanks.

Again, the motivation was the threat of Japanese attack and the disruption of Alaska's supplies. The so-called Canol project turned out to be more difficult to engineer than the highway, and it was two years before the pipeline was operational. By that time the threat of Japanese attack was less serious, and the Canol line was not needed.

While trucks ford a river, American forces build a log bridge as part of their highway to Alaska.

A flotilla of sailboats and a miniature sternwheeler towing a raft rush to a new gold strike on the Fiftymile river downstream of Dawson City in 1898.

some to sail upstream from Dawson, and returned to St. Michael. Those with shallow enough draft sailed up to the Whitehorse rapids, and began transporting both freight and passengers. With the completion of the White Pass railroad in 1900, a navigation pattern was set that would last for 50 years.

The early riverboats were small, and had room only for a few passengers and the wood they burned to make steam. Cargo was loaded on to barges that the boats pushed ahead of them, attached by cables on each side and cleverly manoeuvred around sharp bends and over difficult rapids.

Soon a boatyard was established in Whitehorse, and larger sternwheelers were built. Their draft was so shallow that it was said they could float on dew. Woodcutters toiled all winter to provide their fuel, logs trimmed to the skippers' specifications and stacked in high piles along the riverbank.

As years passed and the Yukon's population declined, only a hard core of larger riverboats remained economic. A typical run between Whitehorse and Dawson took them 40 hours, stopping at settlements along the way and at least twice for wood. At each stop passengers could disembark by a gangplank and explore ashore.

For many travellers, the most exciting part of the trip was negotiating the Five Finger rapids below Carmacks, so named because five large rocks protruded from the water. The sternwheeler had to aim for the largest of these rocks, and at the last moment the current caught the vessel and steered it safely through.

Travelling upstream, the current was so strong that boats needed to attach themselves to a cable and winch themselves up through the rapids. Many sternwheelers came to grief at the Five Fingers or at other reefs or submerged rocks that made every voyage a test of the captain's skill and nerves.

Of course, river traffic could operate

only while the river was free of ice. During the winter, the White Pass and Yukon route offered a stagecoach service between Whitehorse and Dawson. Roadhouses were about 40 km apart, and the trip took between five and seven days. Relays of four or six horses pulled sleighs when there was snow on the ground and wheeled coaches when there was not.

Most of the Klondike's miners departed, and their claims were swallowed up by the huge gold dredges that now dominated the creeks. By the end of World War I Dawson's population was only a fraction of what it had been, and riverboat traffic was in serious decline. Then new deposits of silver, lead, and

zinc were found up the Stewart river.

The discovery set off a minor staking rush to Keno Hill near Mayo, and that meant new business for the riverboats. Not only were they needed to carry supplies, but ore from the mines had to be transported to the railhead at Whitehorse and over the mountains to the coast.

The riverboats sailed on until the early 1950s, when they were made redundant by all-weather roads. Ore from Keno Hill and other sources could now be transported by truck regardless of the season. One by one the riverboats were withdrawn from service, and in 1955 *SS Klondike II* made the final voyage and was pulled from the water.

The steamer *White Horse* negotiates the Five Finger rapids, one of the trickiest hazards on the Yukon river.

ROAD AND RAILROAD

The Alaska highway was built in a hurry and intended only for military vehicles. In 1946 the United States turned it over to the Canadian army, but already it was being used by private trucks and buses travelling between Whitehorse and northern British Columbia.

The highway was earning its keep, and the Canadian army began to improve it. Some sections needed widening, some straightening, some flattening,

A network of highways spans the wide distances between Yukon communities. Only Old Crow in the north is not linked with the system.

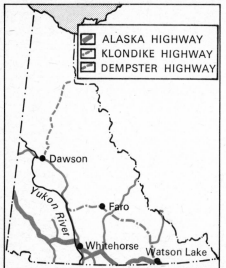

Dust flies as a heavy truck rides gravel on the Klondike highway between Whitehorse and Dawson.

and many of the bridges had to be replaced. There was not enough traffic to justify paving the highway, but it was to be surfaced with gravel and kept open in all seasons.

There was no spectacular increase in road traffic until the early 1950s, when an all-weather road was built to link Mayo and Whitehorse. Ore trucks ran a shuttle service between the mines and the railhead, and the road was soon extended to Dawson — the basis of the Klondike highway of today.

In the 1960s roads were built to serve the large lead-zinc mine opened at Faro near Ross River, and the highway network was improved to help rising numbers of tourists. The Klondike highway has now been extended southwards to Skagway, but the section is open only during summer.

In the north, construction crews have built the Dempster highway to link Dawson with Fort McPherson and Inuvik on the Mackenzie delta. It is the western arctic's sole road link with the rest of Canada, but it is open only during summer. Yukoners fear that unlimited winter traffic might interrupt the migration of the Porcupine caribou herd.

Specially designed containers are used to haul ore concentrate from the Anvil lead-zinc mine at Faro to rail yards near Whitehorse. The containers are carried to Skagway and the ore is shipped to customers in Japan and Europe.

Twin locomotives haul the narrow-gauge cars of the White Pass and Yukon Route on their journey between Whitehorse and the sea.

In spite of the improved highways, most freight entering and leaving the Yukon still goes by way of the White Pass and Yukon rail route across the mountains. Lead and zinc ore is trucked to Whitehorse from the mines and railed to Skagway. Supplies are shipped to Skagway from Vancouver, then railed to Whitehorse for distribution.

Most freight travelling by the White Pass route is carried in containers, a mode of transportation pioneered in the Yukon and now adopted worldwide. Once 'stuffed' into a container, the cargo need not be disturbed from source to destination, which virtually eliminates the risk of damage or pilfering.

The containers have standard dimensions, and can quickly be transferred from ship to truck or train or vice versa. In 1955 the White Pass route took delivery of the world's first ship especially designed to carry containers, and introduced the world's first fully integrated ship-truck-train container system.

Today, the White Pass route operates two container ships travelling between Skagway and Vancouver. Most of the route's revenue comes from ore concentrates, and there has been concern about its future as some mines have stopped producing and cargo tonnage has dropped significantly.

For many years the White Pass route has operated a minor pipeline from Skagway to Whitehorse, bringing in petroleum products. In 1978 the United States and Canada decided to approve a major pipeline built along the route of the Alaska highway, carrying natural gas from Alaska to British Columbia and points to the south.

In part, the route of the proposed pipeline follows that of an old line that carried jet fuel to Fairbanks from Haines on the Alaska coast. It is possible that a lateral pipeline will be built to tap basins of natural gas in the Mackenzie delta and perhaps in the Yukon too, following the route of the Dempster highway.

At the height of summer, a ferry carries traffic across the Yukon river at Dawson. In winter vehicles drive across the ice.

Aviation

The first aircraft seen in the Yukon arrived in the 1920s, and bush pilots soon proved their worth in providing rapid access to the interior. In 1934 two flying-boats were introduced, and provided scheduled services between the Yukon and outside.

As in other parts of Canada, aircraft tended to rely on floats and skis rather than wheels, and the Yukon's lakes and rivers were its only landing places until World War II. Crews building the Alaska highway multiplied the population, and aircraft were used extensively to ferry personnel and carry in needed supplies.

Today, Whitehorse is the Yukon's chief aviation centre, linked with points east, west, north, and south. CP Air connects both Whitehorse and Watson Lake with airports in British Columbia and Alberta, while Transair of Manitoba provides a regular service between Whitehorse, Yellowknife, and Winnipeg.

Smaller northern communities in the Yukon are served by Northward Airlines, and Wien Air Alaska flies between Whitehorse and Fairbanks. For many of the carriers, tourists bound for the Yukon provide a major portion of their revenue, and scheduled services are well supported by a number of small charter operators flying floatplanes and helicopters.

MINING TODAY

As for so long, the mining industry is the Yukon's chief wealth provider. One mine alone is said to account for up to 40 per cent of the territory's total earnings. The industry as a whole justifies many services that would otherwise not exist.

The mine that earns so much is an open-pit lead-zinc producer in the Anvil mountains, a heavily mineralized zone about 200 km north-east of Whitehorse. Developed in the early 1960s, the Anvil mine is expected to have a long life and to be the first of several base metals mines in the area.

Anvil employees live in Faro, a

The concentration plant at Anvil mine. Ore from the benches is crushed and milled and much of the waste rock is removed before the concentrate that survives is trucked to Whitehorse.

townsite some distance from the mine and positioned to serve new mines when and if they are developed. Like other parts of the world, the Yukon is at the mercy of fluctuating base metals prices, and only when markets are profitable can new mines be justified.

Lead and zinc are the Anvil mine's most valuable products, but it holds gold and silver too. The ore is concentrated at the mine, then trucked to Whitehorse, railed to Skagway, and shipped to export markets. Silver, lead, and zinc ores from the mine at Keno Hill follow the same route.

Keno Hill was originally developed as a silver prospect in the years following World War I. Production steadily dropped until the site was nearly abandoned during World War II, but then base metals became more valuable. A new company was formed to work the

A group of miners at Keno Hill, once worked for silver alone but now producing lead and zinc as well.

Staking a Claim

Yukon mining law has changed little since the days of the gold rush. Placer mining (of unconsolidated minerals) is regulated under an act passed in 1906. Quartz or hard rock mining (of minerals still contained in the 'mother lode') falls under an act passed in 1924.

To stake a placer claim, a miner needs two posts, each 10 cm square and 1.2 m tall. These he erects 500 ft. (c. 152 m) apart on the ground he is claiming. Both must be inscribed with the name of the claim, the prospector's name, the date, and the distance between the posts.

With his posts in place, the prospector visits a mining recorder and declares the position of the claim. If it is approved, he pays $10 and is given metal registration tags that he nails to his posts. He then has one year to complete $200 worth of work on the claim, or it reverts to the Crown.

The placer claim gives the prospec-

tor rights over eight hectares of ground, a rectangular shape stretching about 300 m on each side of the line between his posts. The law does not require a miner to declare how much his placer claim produces, or even to pay royalties except on gold that he takes out of the Yukon.

Quartz prospecting is similar except that the area of the claim can be up to 20 ha. A prospector must do at least $100 worth of work on his claim every year, or must pay that amount instead. During each period of 12 months he is allowed to stake up to eight claims within a distance of 16 km from any other mineral claim he holds.

In many cases placer claims and quartz claims overlap one another. Placer miners work surface alluvial deposits while a mining company works underground. In all there are some 5000 placer claims registered in the Yukon, compared with about 44 000 hard rock claims, most of them held by mining companies.

Placer miners continue to work Yukon creeks like their predecessors in the days of the gold rush.

Heavy equipment is used to drill holes for explosives at surface workings of the copper mine near Whitehorse.

deposits and has been in operation ever since.

Unlike the Anvil, Keno Hill is worked underground as miners follow veins containing silver, lead, zinc, and cadmium. That is a method used at Whitehorse copper, an underground mine within Whitehorse's city limits that is also worked from the surface. Besides copper, the mine yields gold and silver as byproducts.

Unfortunately, Whitehorse's deposits are close to exhaustion and the mine will have to close. Even more disappointing, a large asbestos mine developed at Clinton Creek north-west of Dawson closed in 1978 after only ten years in operation. Miners' accommodation was temporary, and not even a ghost town survives their passing.

There is a resurgence of placer mining of gold in the Yukon, particularly around Dawson. However, operations are seasonal and most involve only a few people. In some cases placer miners are recovering other metals besides gold, for instance tungsten and in rare cases platinum.

FORESTS AND FARMS

Base metals and the Yukon's other minerals are non-renewable. Once they are gone, they are gone. However, the Yukon does have resources that can be renewed — trees, water, wildlife, and not least the soil.

A good four million hectares of the territory are covered by productive forest, and another 70 000 ha of forest are potentially productive. As yet, how-

Forest industries use only a fraction of the Yukon's annual growth. The total forest inventory is being checked to see how much more can be cut without hurting the environment.

Tourism

Yukoners have long understood the benefits of looking after travellers. At the time of the gold rush, more fortunes were made by hoteliers, saloon-keepers, and transporters than by the sourdoughs — particularly as miners who struck lucky liked to go on a spree and blow their wealth to the winds.

Long since, the hospitality industry turned from miners to tourists, and tourism is now the Yukon's second largest revenue earner. Many of the Yukon's visitors are in transit between Alaska and the south, but even so, most spend several days in the territory and take the opportunity of looking around.

Most of the visitors arrive by car or camper, travelling the Alaska highway. Some come by air, and a large number arrive by train from Skagway, having cruised the inside passage along British Columbia's coast. Some even arrive on foot, climbing the Chilkoot pass in the steps of the sourdoughs and hiking to Lake Bennett.

Of all the Yukon's attractions, Dawson is inevitably the most glamorous. Parks Canada has restored many of its buildings as part of a national historic park shared with the United States, and there is entertainment at night with gambling at Canada's only legal casino, Diamond Tooth Gertie's.

Most visitors reach Dawson by road, but many prefer to go by river. The adventurous canoe, and the less energetic travel more elegantly in motor cruisers. On the way are historic sites like Fort Selkirk, the Hudson's Bay Company post originally established by Robert Campbell in 1844.

The Kluane National Park in the St. Elias mountains lies beside the Alaska highway and is an easy detour for travellers bound to and from Alaska. The White Pass and Yukon Route railroad offers a day-long journey from Whitehorse to Skagway through some of North America's most exquisite scenery.

Inevitably, most tourist traffic reaches the Yukon during summer, when days are long and skies are clear. Increasingly, the industry has been looking for ways to extend its season. One way is to attract business conventions to Whitehorse, which has a range of hotels and other facilities well able to handle requirements.

Another way is to celebrate the off-season, not least the five months of winter. Enterprising travel agents organize package ski tours and journeys by dog-team. In February Whitehorse hosts the Sourdough Rendezvous, a week-long festival under clear blue skies that show spring cannot be far away.

Otter Falls on the Aishihik river, a well-known beauty spot that is now part of a hydroelectric scheme. Normally the river is diverted away from the falls, but to satisfy tourists, they are permitted to flow in daylight hours during summer.

ever, forest industries are limited to a large sawmill at Watson Lake, three smaller ones near by, and a dozen portable mills that operate in other areas.

The sawmills produce lumber, mine timber, building logs, fence posts, and other products used locally, but take only a fraction of the saw timber volume available. Recent assessments show that the Yukon's forests could be used far more extensively — even to the point of supplying the needs of two pulpmills.

Foresters used to assume that northern forests were too fragile to support full-scale industries. In the Yukon, they find that in some areas trees grow relatively quickly — particularly those in river valleys and on mountain slopes that catch adequate rainfall, at least when their roots are not invaded by permafrost.

Even without forest industries, the trees must be protected. Air patrols and tower lookouts watch for signs of smoke, and alert air tankers and ground crews by radio. A Yukon innovation is the use of tankers to drop chemicals that set backfires, sucked into the main fire by fierce indrafts and slowing or checking its progress. The idea has been taken up by forest services across Canada and in the United States too.

Fortunately for fire-fighters, the Yukon has no shortage of water. Its lakes are a tourist attraction, and its rivers may be the key to the territory's future. Some hydro power has already been harnessed to generate electricity, but it represents only a fraction of the potential.

At present, there are hydro dams on the Yukon river at Whitehorse and on the Aishihik river nearly 140 km to the west. Six more potential dam sites have been identified, and could be used to generate power for new mines, smelters, and perhaps new forest industries.

Furbearers like beaver, muskrat, and fox have been trapped since the days of the Russian fur trade, and trapping is still a way of life for many Yukoners. On rivers of the interior, commercial fishermen catch salmon in nets and Yukon fishwheels — wire scoops mounted on a paddlewheel rotated by the action of the water.

There has been small-scale farming in the Yukon since the days of the gold

John Hatch

rush. Near-continuous daylight compensates for the short growing season, and the chief difficulty for local farmers is lack of precipitation and inadequate processing facilities. Vegetables and some livestock are produced for the local market, but the Yukon is far from self-sufficient and imports most of its food from the south.

On the Yukon river, fishermen construct a salmon fishing wheel that catches fish on paddles and ladles them into nets.

A fine crop of vegetables in Dawson suggests that the Yukon's agricultural production could be much greater than it is.

John Hatch

COMMUNITIES

For most of its length, the Alaska highway is bare of billboards or any other signs. Then travellers reach Watson Lake, and are confronted by what is

A few of the signposts at Watson Lake, one of the most curious sights along the Alaska highway. The collection includes signs from all over North America, nailed up by travellers who have passed that way since 1942.

probably the largest display of road signs in all of North America.

Nobody remembers who nailed up the first of Watson Lake's signs. It was probably a homesick American soldier during World War II, for Watson Lake was the site of a busy construction camp. At all events, the example was soon copied, and signs from all over the continent were carried to the Yukon and nailed up beside the highway.

Even today, the tradition continues.

Young Kutchin Indians port fuel drums at Old Crow, the Yukon's most northerly community.

Motorists who discover that their home town is not represented carry a sign with them and erect it alongside the hundreds of others that are already in place. Each year new stakes are added to carry fresh trophies, and the signs have become a leading tourist attraction.

The Alaska highway has been the making of Watson Lake, which is the

The Population

According to Statistics Canada's mini-census of 1976, Whitehorse had 13 045 inhabitants out of the Yukon's total of 21 836. Other communities had populations as follows:

Faro	1519
Watson Lake	1073
Dawson City	822

third largest community in the Yukon. It has forest industries of its own and is the chief distribution centre for the eastern Yukon and for mines in northern British Columbia and the far west of the Northwest Territories.

Whitehorse too has profited from the highway. Before World War II it was little more than a staging post on the route between Dawson and Skagway, as passengers and freight were transferred from train to riverboat or vice versa. The Alaska highway turned it into a crossroads, and an airport was built there too.

In 1953 Whitehorse became the Yukon's capital at the expense of Dawson, and its prestige has been growing ever since. The rapids that suggested its name lie deep under a hydro reservoir, but an old log church and highrise log cabins rub shoulders with more modern buildings and remind new arrivals that Whitehorse has a past.

Whitehorse remains small — even if it does contain more than half of Yukon's population — but it has become a small town with a big town mentality. The nearest centres of any size are more than 1200 km away, so stores are unusually well stocked. Besides, hotels and restaurants can cater not only to occasional travellers but to whole conventions.

Much of Whitehorse's population is temporary, and there are constant comings and goings. A high proportion of the residents work in government, whether federal or territorial, and between them represent every part of Canada. In summer the population is swelled by the arrival of travellers and tourists from the world outside.

Whitehorse's single most exciting tourist attraction is the elegant hull of the *Klondike II*, the largest and most beautiful of the Yukon riverboats and the last to make a voyage between Dawson and

Whitehorse. She was withdrawn from service in 1955, and today the river route to Dawson is seldom used except by canoeists.

Dawson's resident population is a fraction of what it was at the height of the goldrush. Some estimates suggest that at one point it was as high as 30 000, though that included transients and miners in from their claims. In summer some of Dawson's old glamour is revived as tourists throng its streets or gamble in the casino.

Faro, the Yukon's second largest community, takes its name from a card game popular with the miners of old. It was developed in the early 1960s to accommodate miners working at the nearby Cyprus Anvil lead-zinc mine, and is linked with Whitehorse by all-weather roads much used by convoys of huge trucks.

With the *SS Klondike* high on the Yukon riverbank, Whitehorse basks in the sunlight of a fine winter's day.

Elsa and Mayo are old mining towns in the Keno Hill area east of Dawson, linked with the Klondike highway that connects Dawson and Whitehorse. Carmacks north of Whitehorse is a coal-mining town, and Old Crow far to the north is the only Yukon community not linked with the territory's highway system.

For many visitors, a highlight of the Yukon is Carcross on Bennett Lake, the site where engineers drove the last spike of the White Pass railroad. Carcross still looks much as it did in 1900, and its cemetery is the last resting-place of three of those who discovered the Klondike's gold — Skookum Jim, Tagish Charley, and Kate Carmack.

GOVERNMENT

The most impressive building in Whitehorse is the one that houses the territorial government. Light, airy, and completed in the 1970s, it is the home of the territorial council, the administration, the Yukon archives, and the Whitehorse public library.

The Yukon has been a territory in its own right since 1898, when the Canadian government separated it from the rest of the Northwest Territories. William Ogilvie was appointed the first permanent commissioner or governor, and he and two senior officials sent from Eastern Canada comprised the first Yukon council.

From the start the council was empowered to make local laws and regulations, even though they were subject to Ottawa's approval — still the case today. However, Yukon miners distrusted the abilities of officials fresh to the territory, and demanded and won the right to elect two additional councillors of their own.

Gradually the size of the council was increased, until by 1910 it included ten members. Then the Yukon's population dropped, and by 1919 the council's membership had slumped to three. That was the position until 1952, when the number rose to five. In 1971 it went up to seven, and in 1974 to 12.

In 1978 the number was raised to 16, and for the first time since World War I an election was fought on party lines, with the Progressive Conservatives obtaining a majority. The council elects a speaker, and its proceedings appear to be much like those of the legislative assemblies in the provinces.

Before 1970, the council's chief responsibility was to 'advise' the commissioner, who could accept or reject the advice as he thought fit. The council had no direct influence over the administration, which was headed by an executive committee consisting of the commissioner and other appointed officials.

The single administrative power held by the council was its capacity to refuse approval of the commissioner's budget. To make sure the administration had

The Yukon's legislative council in session. The territorial election of 1978 was fought on party lines, and the 'government' sits to the right of the speaker.

support in the council, in 1970 two members of the council were invited to join the executive committee, and soon a third was added.

Today, five members of the council serve on the executive committee, together with the commissioner and his or her deputy. Following the 1978 election the five members were nominated by the leader of the party that had a majority in the council, and the precedent will probably be followed.

Early in 1979, the federal government appointed a woman, Ione Christensen, as commissioner of the Yukon. The minister of Indian and northern affairs sent her a detailed letter of instructions, making it clear that the department wanted the Yukon to proceed towards full responsible government like that of a province.

Already, the five elected members of the executive committee head departments of the administration. Their re-

Whitehorse and Ottawa

Before introducing new legislation to the legislative council, the Yukon's executive committee must send it to Ottawa for review. Usually it is approved, but sometimes it is refused — particularly if it affects the territory's constitution as set out in the Yukon Act.

The federal government maintains a relatively low profile in the Yukon, its offices distant from the centre of Whitehorse and its activities given much less publicity that those of the territorial government. Even so, it has the final say, and keeps a close eye on the position of Indians and Métis in the territory.

The chief arm of the federal government in the Yukon is the Department of Indian Affairs and Northern Development. Most decisions are taken by officials on the spot, but to their occasional dismay, some are reserved for officials based far away in Ottawa who have limited contact with the situation.

In the territorial government, both the commissioner and deputy commissioner are federal appointees, but in recent years Ottawa has been naming Yukoners to the posts. Otherwise, Yukoners' only input into federal government is through single representatives in the Senate (since 1975) and in the House of Commons (since 1902).

sponsibilities include education, health and welfare, local government, tourism, economic development, administration of justice, highways, and many other fields.

The commissioner retains charge of the Yukon's treasury and of personnel management in the administration. The deputy commissioner is responsible for certain internal government services. Otherwise the elected members are answerable to the full council just like

The territorial government building is one of the most handsome in Whitehorse. It houses the territorial council, public service, and archives, and also the Whitehorse public library.

the cabinet ministers in provinces of the south.

As the executive committee and the administration mature, Ottawa is increasing their responsibilities and interfering less in their decision-making. In time, the influence of the appointed officials will probably be eroded still further, and elected committee members will be responsible for all aspects of the administration.

One crucial difference between territories and provinces is in the ownership of natural resources. At present, the Yukon's belong not to Yukoners but to all the people of Canada — administered from Ottawa and by federal offi-

Whitehorse is a capital city, and a high proportion of residents work for the federal and territorial governments.

cials appointed to the Yukon. There is no prospect of ownership being transferred until Indian land claims have been settled.

During the 1960s the government of British Columbia led by W. A. C. Bennett invited the Yukon to apply for amalgamation with B.C., which would have given it provincial status by adoption. Yukoners have shown little interest in such proposals, for many of them feel that the territory deserves to be a province in its own right.

EDUCATION

The Yukon's small population includes only a few thousand children of school age, and that makes the school system expensive. The student-teacher ratio in Yukon schools has been the lowest in Canada, and costs per pupil are probably the highest.

The Yukon's first schools started in 1898 — one in Dawson and two others accommodated in tents out on the creeks. By 1902 there were so many children in Dawson that a high school was established, with its curriculum and most of its staff drawn from Ontario.

Smaller schools were established in Whitehorse and elsewhere, but until World War II Dawson remained the chief educational centre. Now two-thirds of the Yukon's students are in Whitehorse, which contains ten of the 25 schools in the territory. The others range from fairly large establishments in Faro and Watson Lake to the single-teacher school in Beaver Lake that has fewer than 20 students.

All but three of the schools are run by the territorial government, assisted by advisory school committees. Two separate schools in Whitehorse cater to Roman Catholics and are funded by the

A convoy of buses ferries students between home and school. In Whitehorse, many students from out of town board in special residences.

government, and there is an independent school for Indians at Burwash Landing on Kluane Lake.

Since 1932 the Yukon's education system has been based on British Columbia's rather than Ontario's. Students can progress from kindergarten as far as university entrance. Some of those living in remote areas take B.C. correspondence courses, and some board in Whitehorse and attend school there.

Beyond high school, the territory has a technical and vocational training centre in Whitehorse, established in 1963. The centre offers pre-apprenticeship courses in mechanical, electrical, and construction trades, and also trains assistant nurses and teachers for Yukon schools.

The territory is too small to have a university of its own, but many Yukoners take University of Alberta credit courses by correspondence. Besides, the Yukon government pays the fees of students attending university wherever it may be, and also pays for their transport as far as Edmonton or Vancouver and back.

Besides academic courses, this secondary school in Whitehorse offers technical courses in trades like carpentry, automotive mechanics, and metalwork.

Health Care

The dry climate and an energetic lifestyle keep most Yukoners fit and strong, but there are arrangements for when things go wrong. Five communities have their own small hospital or nursing station, and more serious cases can be treated in Whitehorse or in cities to the south.

The Whitehorse general hospital has 120 beds with two surgeons, a gynecologist, and a psychiatrist in attendance. Outside specialists are brought to Whitehorse for week-long clinics, and emergency cases occurring between their visits can be air-lifted to them in Vancouver or Edmonton.

Until recently Yukon health services fell within federal jurisdiction, though the territorial government paid for them through hospital insurance and medicare. Now the jurisdiction may be transferred to Whitehorse, though the federal government will continue to share the cost of hospital construction.

The Yukon has had hospital insurance since 1960, and medicare since 1972. In addition it operates a 'travel for medical treatment' plan, by which

Whitehorse General Hospital is the Yukon's chief health care facility. The hospital has several specialists on staff, and others based in Vancouver and Edmonton make regular visits.

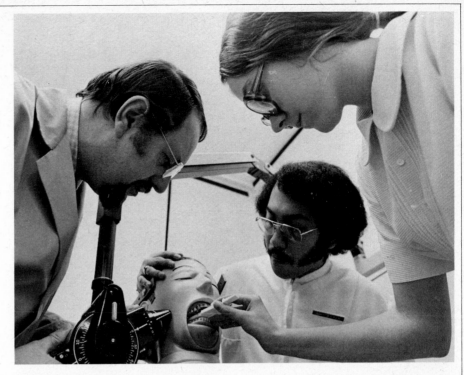

patients contribute no more than $100 towards the cost of transporting them to the nearest point where treatment is available, perhaps Whitehorse but commonly Vancouver or Edmonton.

In 1962 the Yukon established a free dental care program in public schools, the first of its kind in Canada. At first only the youngest children were treated, but now the program extends to Grade 8 and will eventually reach Grade 12. Yukon dental hygienists are trained for two years at Fort Smith in

Student technicians are taught the elements of dentistry in Fort Smith, Northwest Territories, before conducting clinics in the Yukon.

the Northwest Territories.

The dental scheme is an example of preventive medicine, a matter of enhancing health so that potential patients have less opportunity to become sick. The idea has become important all through the health delivery system, not least because it keeps hospital beds free for those who really need them.

THE YUKONERS

There are two great celebrations in the Yukon. Dawson observes 'Discovery Day' in August, and Whitehorse's 'Sourdough Rendezvous' continues for a whole week late in February. Both give visitors the chance to see something of 'the real Yukon.'

Of course, many of those taking part in these festivals are Yukoners only by adoption — but that is typical of 'the real Yukon.' More than half of Whitehorse's population consists of short-term residents, whether individuals or families, yet most of them quickly adapt to the territory's special atmosphere.

Before reaching the Yukon, many visitors picture its inhabitants as long-bearded loners who live in remote log

Outsiders picture Yukoners as prospectors in the wilds, and there are enough left to give substance to the dream.

Indian Rights

In much of Southern Canada, Indians' rights to land were extinguished when their representatives signed treaties with the Canadian government. In the Yukon that did not happen. Indians were too few and it seemed that there was abundant room for all.

In 1902 a Yukon chief offered to negotiate a land treaty at a bargain price, but was ignored. Indians saw the land excavated, trees cut down, and the value of their old hunting and trapping grounds steadily reduced. Now they want compensation for past abuses, and guarantees for their future security.

Some 6000 Yukoners regard themselves as Indian, and their demands extend much further than the cash and land settlements that the Canadian government has conceded in other parts of the country. Yukon Indians want a government of their own, parallel with that of the whites, and a share in controlling all the Yukon's resources.

As the Indians see it, the territorial government does not understand their special way of life. They want control of both primary education and social services on their land, and a full say in secondary education. More startling, they want sole control of the Yukon's renewable resources, as they believe white men lack the experience to administer them properly.

Indian rights have become the most important political issue in the Yukon. The Indians will negotiate only with the federal government, for they will not accept that the territorial government has any power over them. They have said that they will not allow work on the Alaska pipeline to proceed until their demands have been met.

Some 3000 Yukoners count themselves Indians, and many are prominent in the life of the Yukon community. This is a staking party, claiming large areas of the central Yukon on behalf of a mining corporation.

cabins, fishing and trapping and panning gravel from the creeks. Only rarely would such men visit a town, and when they do it is to go on a spree until all their money is spent.

The image has helped the Yukon's tourist industry, and not a few Yukoners try to live up to it — even if their houses have all modern conveniences, they drive fast cars, and they earn their living from conventional jobs. The pioneer spirit comes to the surface at such times as the Rendezvous, when Klondike euphoria fills the air.

In a sense, each year's Rendezvous begins on New Year's Day. That is when contestants in the beard-growing contest appear before the judges with their chins clean-shaven. They will be reassessed seven weeks later, and prizes will be awarded for beard length, bushiness, and sheer menace.

During Rendezvous, sourdoughs who appear in public without beards may be fined by special police who patrol the streets. Worse, they may be locked in a mobile cage and towed around Whitehorse for all to see. The same fate awaits females who fail to wear a garter above the knee.

Snowshoe racing, tug-o'-war contests, whipsaw and wood-chopping competitions, and hill-climbs all have their place in Rendezvous. The strongest take part in a flour packing contest, carrying successively heavier packs for at least 33 m. The swiftest race dog teams on the frozen Yukon river.

Rendezvous is welcome to all because it is a break from the gloomy months of winter. In spite of television

and a generous range of hobbies, Yukoners do suffer from cabin fever, like the sourdoughs before them. Rendezvous gives them a chance to let off steam.

Whitehorse's winter festival is matched by more modest celebrations elsewhere — among them Faro's 'Ice Worm Squirm' and Carmacks' 'Winterlude.' However, it is in summer that the Yukon springs to life. Daylight hours are so long that sourdoughs used to claim hens forgot to lay.

Dawson's Discovery Day has been celebrated since the early days of the century, and today it is a holiday all over the territory. In the past it was a huge family picnic in the open air, but rowdyism among visitors from outside has forced the organizers to hold many of the events indoors.

Old-style sports like climbing a

A three-day dog race on the Yukon river is a highlight of Whitehorse's annual Sourdough Rendezvous.

greasy pole make Discovery Day something to remember, but its climax is a 14-km raft race on the Klondike river. Dawson now spreads its celebration throughout the summer season, from a drama festival in spring to an international outhouse race in September.

Special events like these spice the Yukon's calendar, and help to keep the sourdough spirit alive. That spirit tends to spill over into everyday life, for Yukoners work hard and play hard like the pioneers before them.

Each summer, Yukoners and visitors try their luck in Canada's only legal gambling casino, Diamond Tooth Gertie's in Dawson.

THREE WRITERS

Outsiders' ideas about the Yukon have been influenced by the work of three writers. One was in the territory during the gold rush, one just missed it, and the third was born long after it was all over.

The writer who took part in the gold rush was Jack London, a young Californian who had already wandered all over North America in search of adventure. Grubstaked by his stepsister, he set out for the Klondike in 1897 at the age of 22, spent the winter in a cabin on the Stewart river, and reached the Klondike the next spring.

Jack London never did stake a claim on the goldfields, but he did take a variety of jobs that brought him into contact with the colourful personalities who were the making of the stampede. He absorbed wonderful stories, some based on fact and many the products of fertile imaginations, and within a year returned south to begin setting them on paper.

His success was instant. First short stories, then novels were taken up by publishers and were welcomed not only in North America but in many other countries too. For many readers, Jack London *was* the Yukon — particularly after they read *The Call of the Wild,* the best and most successful of his books and based on a true story.

Robert Service, the second of the Yukon's writers, was in California and elsewhere on the Pacific coast while the stampede was in progress. Service was originally from Scotland, and had worked in a bank before emigrating to Canada to work on a ranch. The life was not as romantic as he had expected, and he drifted in and out of many occupations.

In 1903 Service applied to join a bank once more, and was posted to Whitehorse. There he wrote *Songs of a Sourdough,* among them his famous *The Shooting of Dan McGrew* and *The Cremation of Sam McGee* — Kipling-esque ballads that captured the Yukon's special flavour and remain the most quoted poems ever written about Canada.

In 1908 Service was transferred to Dawson, and there he wrote *Ballads of a Cheechako.* Both his books sold well, and he resigned from the bank and bought himself an old log cabin high on the Dawson hillside. He next wrote a novel of the gold rush, *The Trail of Ninety-Eight,* and it too was a success.

More poems followed, but in 1912 Service accepted a newspaper's invitation to become a war correspondent in the Balkans. He continued to write about the Klondike, but never did he return. Yukoners and outsiders still picture the gold rush through Service's writings — even though he never saw it — and his cabin in Dawson has been preserved as a literary shrine.

The third member of the Yukon's distinguished triumvirate is Pierre Berton, born in Whitehorse in 1920 and brought up in Dawson. By that time Dawson was a shadow of its old self, but surviving sourdoughs told tales of the early days, and Berton later distilled them in best-selling books like his *Klondike.*

Berton left the Yukon while still a boy, and now belongs to all Canada as the contemporary writer who has done most to enhance the nation's heritage. Yukoners appreciate his contributions, but some say that the best book about the territory was written by his mother. Laura Beatrice Berton's *I Married the Klondike* describes life in Dawson from the time she arrived as a young schoolteacher in 1907 until she and her family left for the south in 1932.

Robert Service's cabin in Dawson has become a literary shrine. Ironically, Service's best-known poems of the Klondike were written before he set foot on the goldfields.

The Arts

Each summer, the Yukon's visitors are treated to a revival of vaudeville in Dawson's Gaslight Follies and White-horse's Frantic Follies. Both offerings are re-creations of the kind of entertainment appreciated in the days of the gold rush.

Both shows are professional, but Dawson's is the senior. It has been running longer, and it is staged in the historic Palace Grand Theatre, built in 1899 with timber salvaged from two beached riverboats. There is another live stage show at Dawson's casino, where a resurrected Diamond Tooth Gertie presides as hostess.

Faro is the location of the annual Farrago folk festival, a weekend event that features professional performers brought in from outside the Yukon. Besides appearing on stage, many of the performers lead teaching clinics that help local artists. First held in 1975, the festival attracts Yukoners from all over the territory.

Whitehorse, too, is treated to regular performances by outsiders, among them musicians, puppeteers, dance troupes, and touring theatre companies. On one occasion the whole Victoria Symphony Orchestra was flown in. The capital and many of the smaller communities have well-equipped recreation halls, and amateur productions are well attended.

Two art galleries have opened in Whitehorse in recent years and both feature the work of local artists. Among them are Ted Harrison, whose flat-

The old roadhouse at Carmacks, as drawn by Jim Robb of Whitehorse. A local celebrity little known outside the Yukon, Robb describes his work as 'exaggerated truth, like the poems of Robert Service.'

colour paintings have become popular across Canada, and Jim Robb, whose 'exaggerated truth' as represented in his paintings of decrepit log buildings have won him the reputation of being 'the Robert Service of the easel.'

Can-can dancers of Whitehorse's Frantic Follies, a vaudeville show staged to entertain summer tourists.

THE WILDERNESS

At 6050 m above sea level, Mount Logan in the St. Elias range is the highest mountain in Canada, and a draw for mountaineers from all over North America. Only slightly less popular are Mount Luciana (5325 m) and Mount Steele (5073 m).

All these peaks and several others are within the bounds of one of Canada's newest national parks, Kluane (pronounced Kloo-ah-nee), in the Yukon's south-west corner. In addition, the park contains the world's most extensive

The fireweed, territorial emblem of the Yukon. The flower is the first to bloom in the wake of a forest fire, a symbol of the life that is reawakening.

glaciers outside polar regions.

Kluane covers 22 015 km² of pure wilderness — not mountains and ice-fields alone, but wide valleys, alpine meadows, mountain lakes, tundra, and in places dense vegetation. Besides, it includes a strongly diversified wildlife population, from caribou and moose to grizzly bear and Alaska wolf.

Kluane is easily accessible from the Alaska highway, which makes it a prime-attraction for the Yukon's tourists. An even larger wilderness area, the far north of the territory, is much more difficult to reach — but that suits conservationists who are afraid it may be spoiled.

The northern wilderness represents one of 48 natural regions across the country, as analyzed by Parks Canada. Eighteen of them are at least partially conserved in national parks. Of the remaining 30, at least six are wholly or partly north of the 60th parallel, including the one in the northern Yukon.

One factor that makes the northern wilderness unusually vulnerable is the presence of the huge Porcupine caribou herd, some 110 000 strong and migrating between north-eastern Alaska and parts of the Northwest Territories. The herd's chief calving grounds are in the northern Yukon, on the flatlands close to the coast.

Many other species of wildlife are found in the north, and the coastal region and the wetlands of the Old Crow flats are critical staging and nesting areas for large numbers of water-fowl. Besides, there is a strong population of raptors including eagles, hawks, gyrfalcons, and ospreys.

In 1978 the Canadian government announced that no more resource development would be allowed in the region, apart from prospecting and oil and gas exploration already in progress. The only communities in the area — Old Crow and the harbour on Herschel Island — were excluded too.

The wilderness plan pleased Indian leaders, who had been demanding a halt to development in view of their land claims. The territorial government, however, was not consulted, and was predictably upset. The wilderness will

As if in a painting, the surface of the lake reflects the contours of a lonely peak in the southern Yukon.

Animal Kingdom

Polar bears sport on the shores of the Beaufort sea, and mountain goats perch on precarious ledges high in the St. Elias range. From south to north, the Yukon has an abundant wildlife population that appeals to naturalists, photographers, and hunters.

Polar bears keep to the north, but the rest of the territory contains many black (or brown) bears and a number of grizzly bears too. Timber wolves include the tundra subspecies found north of the Porcupine river and the larger Alaska wolf found all over the territory, but particularly in the west.

There are mule deer in the southern Yukon, and moose are plentiful throughout the interior. Towards the north there are small groups of woodland caribou, and on the tundra roam their cousins of the barren lands, the migratory caribou of the Porcupine herd.

The territory holds several species of mountain sheep — among them the Dall sheep of the north and southwest, nearly pure white, and the dark brown Stone sheep south of the Pelly river. Fannin sheep are white with dark saddles, but all three species intermix.

The Yukon's furbearers include beaver, ermine, mink, marten, muskrat, otter, lynx, and arctic fox. There are red foxes as well, and snowshoe rabbits are common. Porcupines, pikas, and marmots add further variety, and there are many smaller creatures like lemmings, ground squirrels, and meadow mice.

The smaller creatures fall easy prey to the many raptor species found in the Yukon — bald and golden eagles, peregrine falcons, owls, and hawks. Ducks, grouse, ptarmigan, and other game species abound, and there are trumpeter swans, oven birds, Lapland longspurs, northern phalaropes, and long-tailed jaegers too.

Pacific salmon reach Yukon rivers to spawn, and there are trout, whitefish, inconnu, pike, and arctic grayling to tempt northern fishermen. Off the Yukon's coast, there are bowhead whales and beluga white whales, and the Pacific walrus and bearded seals are found there also.

Thinhorn Dall sheep perch in the mountains of the Kluane range in the Yukon's south-west corner.

remain unsullied until Parks Canada decides if and when something should be done with it.

Of course, the Yukon is by no means short of wilderness, even apart from the special reserves. The territory retains its frontier atmosphere in spite of decades of development, and hunters, fishermen, hikers, and photographers flock there from all over the continent and elsewhere.

The Yukon's rivers challenge both canoeists and white-water rafters. Some canoeists have paddled all the way from Whitehorse to the sea, but most content themselves with the 500-km run to Dawson. Rafters brave the rapids of the Klondike river or longer runs on the Yukon or its many tributaries.

Flowing a few metres each year, the majestic glacier carves a path through the St. Elias mountains of Kluane National Park.

NORTHWEST TERRITORIES

The Landforms

The Northwest Territories are made up of at least five main geological components. Three are mountain systems, and the others are a large portion of Canada's Precambrian Shield and the sedimentary plains that overlay it.

The Precambrian Shield consists of a jumble of ancient rocks formed earlier than 600 million years ago. The

A cairn in the rock desert of Keewatin's barren lands, perhaps a memorial or beacon. In the distance, the abandoned huts of an old fur trading post.

rocks provide North America's geological core, and are visible on the surface in a giant horseshoe shape that cradles Hudson Bay. Besides, they underlie the bay and all the N.W.T.'s younger geological features too.

West and north of the Shield are great plains connected with those of Southern Canada. They consist of sediments deposited at the bottom of ancient seas and lakes, among them strata containing precious oil and natural gas. The most recent layers of sediment were laid down in the Tertiary period, around 50 million years ago.

According to recent geological theory, the North American continent rests on a huge, free-floating plate that forms part of the earth's crust. The plate responds to occurrences within the earth's mantle, and moves in relation to neighbouring plates. The pressures generated when plates collide or pull apart can build mountains.

In the N.W.T., geologists identify three separate areas in which moun-

Running as far north as the arctic circle, the Mackenzie mountains divide the Northwest Territories from the Yukon to the west.

tains have been formed. One is the Mackenzie region of the west, part of the Cordillera that extends into the Yukon. A second is southern Baffin Island, where mountains are related to the Appalachian chain that curves southwards to Alabama.

The third mountain system is in the north, the high ranges of northern Baffin Island, Ellesmere Island, and other parts of the arctic archipelago. As in the western Cordillera, crustal plates pushed together and forced sediments high above the sea. Ellesmere Island contains the highest peaks in eastern North America.

Continuing erosion by wind, water, frost, and ice have sculpted the N.W.T.'s landforms. Successive ice ages helped to wear away layers of sediment and break down the mountains, and pushed soil far from its original location. Even today the northern islands retain ice caps and glaciers that are impressive reminders of nature's authority.

THE TREELINE

On the map, the Northwest Territories appear to be cut in half by the imaginary line known as the arctic circle. The line marks the zone in which the sun does not set on at least one day of summer, and does not rise on at least one day of winter.

For geographers, the arctic circle has no other significance. To them, a more important division is the treeline, another imaginary boundary that shows where it becomes too cold for trees to survive. The treeline snakes across the territories from the Mackenzie river delta in the north-west, towards the Hudson Bay coast in the south-east.

North of the treeline stretch vast expanses of arctic tundra. Large areas consist of rock desert that is bare of vegetation except for a short period in summer when tiny flowers bloom. Most of the remainder is covered by grass-like plants, mosses, and lichens that provide fine grazing for herds of caribou and musk oxen.

Some sheltered areas of the tundra support low shrubs like stunted willow, alder, and ground birch. In places, tongues of forest probe northwards from the treeline, as on the Coppermine river and on the barrens west of Baker Lake. The frost-free growing season is short, but while it lasts, there is almost continual sunlight to encourage the varied plant life.

South of the treeline, the tundra scrub is mixed with scattered stands of stunted conifers like spruce and larch. In places there are stands of white birch, one of the few deciduous trees able to withstand the cold climate. The trees grow painfully slowly because the summer is short and precipitation is very limited.

The only densely forested areas of the N.W.T. are south and west of Great Slave Lake, in the lowlands that form the collection basin of the Mackenzie river. The most common trees are spruce, balsam, fir, jackpine, birch, tamarack, and aspen. The soil is not especially fertile, but even so, it could probably be used for agriculture.

One paradox of the N.W.T. is that it receives much less snow than many regions of Southern Canada. North of the treeline, the snow packs hard

enough to be walked on without skis or snowshoes. It blankets the ice of lakes and rivers, and at the coast it conceals the division between land and frozen sea.

The winter is long and cold, but at the same time dry and healthy. When spring comes, there is an immediate transformation. River ice rots and the snow disappears, and the land is revealed as an immense mosaic of tens of thousands of lakes. The great majority are shallow and have no outlet, but some are connected with river systems that stream to the sea.

The most important of these rivers is the Mackenzie, which springs from Great Slave Lake and rolls northward, almost losing itself in a vast delta of muskeg swamp. At Fort Simpson it is joined by the Liard river from British Columbia. At Fort Norman it is connected with Great Bear Lake, 31 080 km² in extent and the fourth largest lake in North America.

Great Slave Lake covers 28 930 km² and is North America's fifth largest lake. Rivers flow into it from several directions, but the most important is the

Forests border the Lockhart river, which empties into the eastern arm of Great Slave Lake.

Slave. Rising from Lake Athabasca on the Alberta-Saskatchewan boundary, the Slave is part of a river system that reaches to the Rocky mountains.

Several rivers help to drain the barren lands. Among them are the Coppermine and the Back, which head for the polar sea. In the Keewatin region west of Hudson Bay, the Thelon and Kazan rivers empty into Baker Lake, which is close to Canada's geographic centre. The lake is at the head of Chesterfield Inlet, a fjord-like arm with access from Hudson Bay.

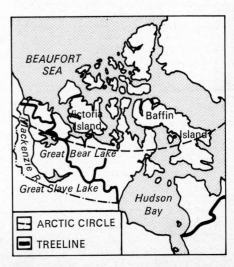

BEAUFORT SEA

Mackenzie

Victoria Island

Baffin Island

Great Bear Lake

Great Slave Lake

Hudson Bay

☐ ARCTIC CIRCLE
▭ TREELINE

The arctic circle that girdles the northern hemisphere is less significant than the treeline, the point at which the climate is normally too severe for trees to survive.

NATIONAL PARKS

In 1978 member nations of Unesco (the United Nations Educational, Scientific, and Cultural Organisation) signed the World Heritage Convention. Their objective was to draw up a list of natural and cultural sites around the world that were of outstanding universal value.

As a start, five natural and eight cultural sites were nominated to the list. The natural sites included the United States' Yellowstone National Park, Ecuador's Galapagos islands, and Ethiopia's Simien National Park. There was also a nomination from Canada — Nahanni National Park in the Northwest Territories.

Ironically, Nahanni is one of Canada's least accessible and least known national parks. It is located in the N.W.T.'s south-west corner, and follows the course of the South Nahanni river. The river's most famous attractions are Virginia Falls, more than twice the height of Niagara Falls, and Pulpit Rock, a vertical cliff 210 m tall that guards a hairpin turn.

Tumultuous rapids, fierce whirlpools, and narrow gorges, like Hell's Gate, make the river a severe test for canoeists. Naturalists enjoy the park's rich vegetation and abundant wildlife, which includes moose, grizzly bear, and woodland caribou. Hot springs create local ecosystems that to the casual eye seem almost tropical.

Set aside in 1971, Nahanni covers an area of 4766 km². Wood Buffalo National Park, south of Great Slave Lake, has an area of 44 807 km², but less than one-third of it is in the N.W.T. with the remainder across the Alberta boundary. The park was set aside in 1922 to protect Canada's last remaining herd of wood buffalo.

Pulpit Rock, a sheer cliff overlooking a hairpin bend in the Nahanni river, is one of the leading attractions of Nahanni National Park.

Virginia Falls on the South Nahanni river are more than twice the height of Ontario's Niagara.

Like Nahanni, Wood Buffalo is a wilderness park. It is accessible from Fort Smith in the N.W.T. and includes a rich wildlife population of both wood and plains buffalo, black bear, moose, and woodland caribou. A special treasure is the nesting ground of the rare whooping crane, just inside the N.W.T.

The third of the N.W.T.'s national parks is Auyuittuq on the north coast of Baffin Island. *Auyuittuq* means 'the place that does not melt,' and the park is a wilderness of jagged mountains and deep fjords surrounding the Penny ice cap and the glaciers it has spawned.

Parks Canada has set aside five more regions of the Northwest Territories as 'natural areas of Canadian significance.' In time they may become national parks. One is tiny, conserving some of the pingos near Tuktoyaktuk — ice blisters rising from the permafrost and covered with soil and vegetation.

The other natural areas are: the north of Banks Island, important as a breeding ground for musk ox and arctic fox; Bathurst Inlet on Coronation Gulf, close to an important caribou migration route; Wager Bay in Keewatin, an oasis in the tundra rich in wildlife; and two areas on Ellesmere and Axel Heiberg islands in the high arctic.

The Wildlife

Forests, barrens, islands, and sea all hold a rich variety of wildlife. Above or below the treeline, mammals and birds are an essential part of the environment, and they comprise the N.W.T.'s most valued resource.

Moose abound in the Mackenzie valley, and there are grizzlies and black bears in the mountains to the west. Beaver, muskrat, and all the other furbearers typical of Canada's boreal forest are present as well. There are wood buffalo south and west of Great Slave Lake, and to the north are woodland caribou.

The woodland caribou differ from their cousins of the tundra, the barren ground caribou. They are larger, they live in small groups rather than in herds, and they are not great travellers. In contrast, each summer the barren ground caribou migrate hundreds of kilometres in herds tens of thousands strong.

Biologists have classified at least seven major caribou herds in the N.W.T., each migrating in a wide circle. The deer come together in April and May, calve in June, and continue migrating until August. In October they mate, and then the herds break into small groups that trail back to their wintering range independently.

The sight of 100 000 migrating caribou is one of the great experiences of the north. Another is to spot a group of musk oxen — the shaggy, shambling beasts that are related to both cattle and goats. Threatened by an aggressor, the musk oxen form into a line or perhaps a circle, and the bulls take turns to charge.

Most of the N.W.T.'s musk oxen are on the islands of the high arctic, but there are small herds at Bathurst Inlet and in the Thelon game sanctuary in the central barrens. Like caribou, musk oxen eat lichens and other plants that they detect by smell, and in winter reach them by pawing through the snow.

Great white wolves prey on the musk oxen and on weaker caribou as well — their only enemies apart from man. Arctic foxes, prized for their snowy pelts, feed on mouse-like lem-

mings that breed prolifically. The barren ground grizzly bear has become so rare as to be almost a memory.

On the coast, polar bears chase seals in the water and on the ice. Walrus, narwhals, and beluga white whales thrive on the rich marine vegetation. Seabirds, geese, swans, and ducks arrive for the summer breeding season, and so do rare birds of prey like peregrine falcons, gyrfalcons, and the snowy owl.

Not many bird species are prepared to remain north for the winter.

Walrus are valuable for their meat and for their ivory tusks, but are protected by strict hunting regulations.

Those that do include the ptarmigan, its plumage white as snow, and the ungainly raven, coal-black and rather sinister. The raven seems so foreign to the north that Inuit used to think of it as a spirit, and it plays a prominent role in their folk traditions.

Musk oxen, related to both cattle and goats, roam the islands of the high arctic and parts of the mainland too.

THE PEOPLE

Inuit apart, the original peoples of the Northwest Territories call themselves the Dene — 'the people.' They belong to six main tribes that are part of the Athapaskan language family, a cultural grouping that is represented from Alaska to New Mexico.

The N.W.T.'s Athapaskans may have entered the region from the Yukon, or may have come from the south. Some archaeologists think both theories are correct. The Mackenzie basin has been occupied by Dene and their forerunners for at least 10 000 years, that being the age of a fishing camp still in use near Fort Liard in the south-west.

The fishing camp was first occupied by a culture identified by its use of small cutting tools made of flint. The people evidently hunted caribou and small game of the forest, but otherwise little is known about them. In about 5000 BC they were joined by buffalo hunters from the south, who used long spears to kill their prey.

The bison people began hunting caribou, and learned to follow their summer migration north to the barren lands. In winter they returned to the forest. Some travelled as far as Keewatin, where the forest grew farther north than it does now. Two of their winter houses have been found — shallow pits that were probably roofed with skins.

In about 1000 B.C. another group of hunters moved north from the plains, trusting in bows and arrows rather than spears. They too hunted bison and caribou and fished in the lakes and rivers. Meanwhile, a prolonged cold spell forced the Keewatin hunters to retreat towards the south.

Steadily the hunters evolved the way of life familiar to the Dene of today. In summer they travelled by canoe. In winter they moved about on snowshoes, towing their possessions on light toboggans. As yet there was no thought of using dog teams to pull sleds, for that was an idea introduced by white men, who borrowed it from the Inuit.

Caribou, moose, beaver, and other prey gave Dene their food, clothing, and the hides they needed for their skin tents. They lived in independent family groups frequently on the move, but remained within the broad area accepted as their tribal homeland. Most groups lived in peace with their neighbours, though there were exceptions.

White men did not enter the north-western forest until the eighteenth century. By then the six tribes recognized today were settled on their hunting grounds. East of Great Slave Lake were the Chipewyan people — 'those with pointed skins,' a reference to the long, pointed coattails they wore both front and back.

The Chipewyans hunted caribou, and each summer those living close to the treeline followed the deer on to the barrens. The same was true of the Dogribs who lived between Great Slave Lake and Great Bear Lake. They took their name from an ancient legend that all men were descended from a dog.

The Slaveys, now the largest of the N.W.T.'s Dene tribes, lived south and west of Great Slave Lake, and concentrated on hunting moose rather than caribou. They were frequently at odds with the Nahanni of the mountain country in the southwest, who hunted both moose and woodland caribou.

The Nahanni spoke the same language as the Loucheux, who lived in the northern mountains and on the Mackenzie delta. To the south were the Hares, so named because they hunted small animals for the pot. A seventh tribe, the Yellowknives, perished of disease in the nineteenth century.

Today, Dene leaders see their people as a nation within Canada. Besides the six surviving tribes, the nation includes mixed-blooded Métis, who are descended from Dene and non-Dene — in most cases whites. The Dene nation insists that it holds aboriginal rights to a large part of the N.W.T. south of the treeline.

Dene afloat on Great Slave Lake, towards the end of the nineteenth century. These Dene are Dogribs, part of the great Athapaskan language family.

Public Archives Canada C-3946

Eskimos and Inuit

Like the Dene, the forerunners of Canada's Inuit seem to have reached North America by way of the Bering strait. Indians of north-eastern Canada referred to them as *eskimo*, 'those who eat raw meat,' and like the Dene regarded them as enemies.

The first *eskimo* were probably only distantly related to the Inuit of today. Archaeologists refer to them as the Denbigh people, who flourished between 3000 BC and 1000 BC. Traces of them have been found from Alaska to Greenland, and from northern Ellesmere Island to Great Slave Lake.

The Denbigh people lived by hunting land mammals, and dwelt in low stone houses roofed by skins. Probably because of a change in climate, they were forced to adapt their lifestyle. Now described as the Dorset people, they lived closer to the coast and hunted seals and walrus. Archaeologists suspect that the Dorset culture invented the snow house.

Dorset *eskimo* flourished between 1000 BC and 1000 AD. Modern Inuit know of them through stories passed down by their ancestors, who originated in Alaska and gradually eliminated the older culture. Known as the Thule people, the newcomers lived in villages rather than as nomads, and specialized in hunting whales.

The Thule people spread across the arctic like the Denbigh culture before them. It was they who introduced dog teams as a mode of transportation, and they had kayaks (hunting canoes for men) and umiaks (transport canoes for women) as well. Some groups deserted the coast and moved on to the barrens, learning to live by the caribou.

Between 1650 and 1850 there was a 'little ice age' in which the Thule people changed their ways. No longer could they live by whaling, and they abandoned their large villages. Instead they became nomads, travelling as small groups and making seasonal camps of tents or snow houses.

So was laid the pattern of life remembered by the Inuit of today. Many still alive were born in snow houses or skin tents, and Inuit still hunt caribou, musk oxen, polar bears, walrus, seals, and beluga whales. Whole families look forward to the summer fishing season, and Inuit women have not lost their skill as tailors of the north.

Early white visitors were fascinated by the snow villages of the Inuit. In many, a number of family dwellings were grouped around a central dancing house.

Public Archives Canada C-21115
Inuit of Baffin Island display their catch of arctic char and an arctic fox, c. 1700.

STRAAT DAVIS en HUDSON

Searching for the Northwest Passage, Martin Frobisher found Baffin Island and went home to England with black rock that was said to contain gold. Frobisher twice returned to his mines before the rock was found to be worthless.

Meta Incognita

In 1576 three tiny ships from England struck boldy across the Atlantic. In command was Martin Frobisher, a former freebooter keen to win fame and wealth by finding a new route to the orient. He dreamed of locating a north-west passage around the top of the New World.

The ships sighted Greenland in July, but in a gale that followed the smallest was lost with all hands. The others were driven north and west, and came to the vast polar region now known as Baffin Island. Frobisher was convinced that it was Asia, particularly when he met fur-clad Inuit who to him looked 'like Tartars.'

Frobisher named his discovery *Meta Incognita*, or 'Unknown Shore.' The two ships returned to England and Frobisher was acclaimed a hero. A piece of black rock obtained on Baffin Island was examined and judged to contain gold. In the next year, Frobisher was sent back to Meta Incognita, this time accompanied by a ship belonging to Queen Elizabeth.

Leading his men ashore with banners unfurled, Frobisher took possession of the land in the queen's name. There were encounters with Inuit, some friendly and some fierce, and the Englishmen laboured to fill their ships with black rock. On the way home the three vessels lost contact, but even so all arrived safely.

By now England was gripped by gold fever. In 1578, Frobisher set sail with 15 ships and an expedition that included professional miners and colonists too. Several separate mines were worked, and with great effort a large quantity of rock was carried to England. To everyone's dismay, it was now shown to be totally worthless.

The riches of Asia seemed as remote as ever. In 1585 a group of English speculators equipped a new expedition to seek a north-west passage. In command was the pilot John Davis, who reached Baffin Island and explored the great strait now named after him. Davis was the first of a score of navigators who helped to fill blanks on the map.

The navigators included Henry Hudson, who in 1610 found the huge bay that bears his name, and William Baffin, perhaps the greatest navigator of all. Baffin's discoveries were not ratified for 200 years, but it was he who discovered Smith Sound, leading to the north pole, and Lancaster Sound, the key to the north-west passage.

Sadly, Baffin failed to realize the significance of Lancaster Sound. Between 1612 and 1616 he had taken part in four expeditions to the northern seas, but then he was appointed pilot of East Indiaman convoys sailing in the spice trade. Fifteen years later Luke Foxe explored the western coast of Hudson Bay and concluded that the north-west passage was a pipedream.

The fjord of Pangnirtung on Baffin Island, which adjoins the *Meta Incognita* discovered by Martin Frobisher in 1576.

COMPANY SERVANTS

Martin Frobisher's expeditions had produced only fool's gold, but the efforts of French adventurers showed that the New World held treasure of a different sort. In 1670 a group of wealthy Englishmen laid plans to develop a northern fur trade from within Hudson Bay.

The Hudson's Bay Company, as the venture came to be called, built a number of forts at the mouths of rivers emptying into the bay. Local Indians were encouraged to trap beaver and other animals. After a period of struggle against French rivals, in the 1730s the English began constructing a huge fortress of stone near what is now Churchill.

Fort Prince of Wales catered to Chipewyan Indians of the interior. In 1768 a party of these Indians brought with them specimens of copper ore from the distant north. The governor of the fort asked permission to send a company servant to visit the region and look for more. Permission was granted, and in 1769 the governor despatched Samuel Hearne.

At this time only 24 years old, Hearne already had a thorough knowledge of Hudson Bay's west coast and of the Indians. It was arranged that he would travel with a group of Indians who were leaving for the west, and would then turn north to seek the river that led to the copper mines.

Unfortunately, Hearne made two false starts. His first trip ended when his Indian guides abandoned him. The second was aborted when his navigation equipment was smashed. Fortunately he then met Mattonabee, a resourceful Chipewyan who had some knowledge of English and who agreed to lead him to the Coppermine river.

Hearne and Mattonabee left the fort late in 1770 and travelled west across the barrens until they came to Wholalich Lake. Then they turned north and west, and reached the Coppermine not far from the sea. To Hearne's lasting disgust, his companions took the oppor-

tunity of massacring a party of unsuspecting Inuit asleep in their camp.

The copper deposits were a disappointment. In spite of a diligent search, only small fragments were found. The party travelled south, giving Hearne the opportunity to see Great Slave Lake and to meet the Dene he named Yellowknives, because they fashioned tools from copper. Only then did Hearne and Mattonabee turn eastwards to regain the fort, where they arrived in June 1772.

Meanwhile, the Hudson's Bay Company had competition. Following Britain's capture of New France in 1760, aggressive fur traders based in Montreal were challenging the company on its own ground. During the 1780s some of them came together as the North West Company, and their representatives travelled as far as the Athabasca country.

One of these traders was Alexander Mackenzie, whose dream was to find a route to the Pacific. According to Indian sources, a great river led westwards from Great Slave Lake. In 1789 Mackenzie reached the lake with a party of voyageurs and Indians, and after two weeks' search located the river now named after him and embarked on it.

Samuel Hearne, the discoverer of the Coppermine river and the first white man to see the inner reaches of the polar sea.

To Mackenzie's disappointment, his river soon turned northwards. Even so, he decided to see where it led — in spite of the protests of his companions. For weeks they paddled onwards, until at last they reached the delta. There Mackenzie mounted a high island — perhaps a pingo — and spotted the distant icefield that covered the polar sea.

Barren ground explorers like Samuel Hearne contended with a bewildering maze of rocks and lakes that stretched to the polar sea.

Public Archives Canada C-1906

NAVAL MEN

In 1818 Britain's Royal Navy sent two expeditions northwards to build on the achievements of earlier explorers. One was to search for the north-west passage, and the other was to sail straight for the north pole.

Not surprisingly, the north pole expedition was a fiasco. It was important only because it was the first arctic experience of John Franklin, the most famous explorer of his generation. The

Capt. John Franklin's two overland expeditions made him famous, but his voyage of 1845 ended in disaster.

Public Archives Canada C-13161

ships searching for the north-west passage were more successful. Under Capt. John Ross they penetrated Lancaster Sound and sailed 80 km inside it.

The success led the navy to try again. Capt. William Parry took two ships through Lancaster Sound, into Viscount Melville Sound, and southwards down Prince Regent Inlet. Had Parry continued, he might have found the passage. Instead he turned back, and his ships were the first to spend a winter locked into the ice of the polar sea.

Meanwhile, John Franklin was engaged on a quite different expedition. With four naval companies and a party of voyageurs, he had ventured inland from Hudson Bay. His instructions were to explore the coastline reached by Hearne and Mackenzie and to discover if navigation was practical in that region of the arctic.

Franklin's route took him to Lake Athabasca on what is now the Saskatchewan-Alberta boundary, and then to Great Slave Lake. The party built winter quarters about 200 km to the north of Great Slave Lake, and in the summer of 1821 canoed down the Coppermine river. At the sea, they turned eastwards and explored the coastline for as long as they dared.

They went too far. By the time they turned back, winter gales were blowing ice against the coast. They had to land and strike south across the barrens. The whole party suffered appalling hardship and several men perished before the survivors reached their old winter quar-

A chance meeting of five ships in Hudson Strait off Baffin Island in 1821. Two were naval (*HMS Hecla* and *HMS Fury*), two belonged to the Hudson's Bay Company, and the fifth was carrying Swiss settlers bound for the Red river colony in what is now Manitoba. A sketch by one of the settlers, Peter Rindisbacher.

ters. Even then, Franklin himself nearly died before they were rescued by Dene trappers.

In spite of the ordeal, in 1825 Franklin and two of his former companions — John Richardson, a surgeon, and the artist George Back — were ready to go on a second expedition. Again they were to fill in blanks on the map, linking what they knew of the west with knowledge recently gained in the east.

Franklin and his men descended the Mackenzie river. At the mouth they divided into two parties. One, led by Richardson, sailed eastwards to the mouth of the Coppermine. Franklin and Back went to the west, to Herschel Island and beyond. They were looking for the naval expedition sent around Alaska to meet them.

The rendezvous was not kept, but Franklin was convinced that the arctic waters were connected with the Pacific. Eastwards, his earlier expedition had reached a point south of Viscount Melville Sound. If he could find a route between the two, a north-west passage would be assured.

In the years that followed, several more naval expeditions visited the

arctic, but each time the passage eluded them. One was led by Capt. James Ross, who took an experimental steamship to Prince Regent Inlet and became stuck in the ice. Ross and his men were marooned for four winters before being rescued by another expedition.

In spite of prodigious efforts, the navy was making little progress. Once more it turned to Franklin, recently returned from Australia. In 1845 Franklin set sail in command of an expedition of two ships, his men hand-picked for their experience of the arctic. The ships first sailed to Greenland, where a supply base was established.

In July of 1845 the ships sailed across Baffin Bay. On board were 129 men, and they had supplies enough to last for three years. Eighteen months elapsed and there was no word for them. On Ross's advice the navy sent a ship to met Franklin in the Bering Strait, in case he was running short of supplies.

By 1848 there was still no word of the expedition. It was feared the ships were stuck in the ice as Ross's had been, and the navy sent another relief expedition. Besides, Franklin's old friend Richardson was in Canada, and travelled down the Mackenzie to look for him in the polar sea.

Meanwhile, public concern was mounting. The navy sent out more ships, and private expeditions went too. Between 1847 and 1851, there were no fewer than 21 separate rescue efforts by land and by sea. Searchers combed the arctic, questioning Inuit as they went, but no trace of Franklin was to be found.

Then at last came positive news. In 1851 one of the expeditions visited Beechey Island north of Lancaster Sound. There it found what must have been Franklin's winter quarters of 1845-1846. Three graves were located, but of ships and men there was no sign.

For a time it seemed possible that Franklin and his men were still alive.

Members of the McClintock relief expedition of 1857 found a cairn on King William Island. In it they found a record of the fate of Franklin's expedition, when 129 men were lost.

Then came word from Dr. John Rae, a distinguished explorer sent overland by the Hudson's Bay Company. Rae had met a party of Inuit, who told him of an encounter several years earlier. They had seen about 40 white men hauling a boat and sleds southwards across the ice of the polar sea.

The white men were thin and weak, and the Inuit supplied them with food. Later in the season they came upon the bodies of many of these men, but not all were accounted for. The Inuit gathered relics left near the bodies, some of them marked with Franklin's initials. Rae obtained many of these relics and forwarded them to London.

Hopes of finding any of the men alive were nearly extinguished. Committed to fighting the Crimean war, the navy gave up its search. Finally a small private expedition sailed in 1857, organized by Capt. Francis McClintock out of compassion for Franklin's grieving widow. Members of his party found a small cairn on King William Island.

Inside the cairn was a document. First placed there in 1847, it reported that all was well with Franklin's men, though the ships were caught in pack ice. But there was more. The cairn had been reopened a year later, and a note had been added. The crews were preparing to abandon their ships.

The location of the cairn proved that Franklin had found his north-west passage. Given more luck, he would have had a clear run to Coronation Gulf and reached points he had explored 40 years earlier. Instead he lost his life in the attempt. According to the note he had died in 1847.

KABLOONA POWER

The Hudson's Bay Company's charter gave it exclusive rights to Rupert's Land, the vast area drained by rivers that emptied into Hudson Bay. In addition, the company controlled a 'North-West Territory,' the Indian country of the Mackenzie valley and the Yukon.

That was the position until 1870, when the holdings were transferred to the young Dominion of Canada. They stretched from the Cordillera to Labrador, from the arctic sea to the 49th parallel. Rupert's Land was partitioned, and the regions south and west of Hudson Bay were renamed 'the North-West Territories.'

In 1880 the territories were made even larger when Britain presented Canada with its arctic islands. Canada did nothing to assert any claim to them, and between 1898 and 1902 Otto Sverdrup claimed parts of the high arctic for Norway. In haste, a Canadian expedition was sent north to make a formal annexation.

Meanwhile, gold had been discovered on the Klondike. In 1898 the Yukon was made a territory in its own right. Besides, in 1899 and 1900 Canadian government agents persuaded Dene living south of Great Slave Lake to sign Treaty No. 8. In doing so, they relinquished their land rights in return for cash and other considerations.

Since 1882, the 'North-West Territories' had been governed from Regina on the prairies. A lieutenant-governor represented the Crown, and a legislative council represented the people. In 1905 Saskatchewan and Alberta became provinces, and after 1912 the Northwest Territories were reduced to what they are today.

No northern community was equipped to become capital of the shrunken territories, so they were ruled from Ottawa. In place of a lieutenant-governor, they were made the responsibility of a part-time commissioner. There was supposed to be an advisory council too, but for 15 years nothing was done about appointing one.

Then in 1920 oil was discovered at Norman Wells on the Mackenzie river. It was Canada's first major oil strike in 60 years. Prospecting crews searched the region for fresh deposits, and government agents persuaded local Dene to sign a second treaty. This one was No. 11, containing much the same terms as No. 8.

Today, Dene dispute the validity of both these treaties. They claim their forebears were misinformed about the contents, and that in any case many of the signatures on them were forged. Whether the treaties were legal or not, there was no move to set aside Indian reservations as had happened in Southern Canada.

Above the treeline, kabloona traders were in the market for arctic fox pelts. Mission stations were established close to fur trading posts, and detachments of the Royal Canadian Mounted Police arrived too. Some of the police were sent to the arctic islands to convince other countries that they were Canadian territory.

In 1930 a prospector found pitchblende at Great Bear Lake. Pitchblende was a source of radium and uranium, and until that time the Belgian Congo had held a monopoly of the world's radium supply. A mine was opened at Port Radium, and other prospectors spread across the north. In 1934 they found gold at Yellowknife on Great Slave Lake.

More and more white men were entering the N.W.T. During World War II Canada and the United States built an airfield at Frobisher Bay on Baffin Island, and several smaller fields elsewhere. After the war, Frobisher Bay became the chief supply base as Canada built a line of defence installations across the arctic.

Starting in the 1950s, the kabloonas set out to improve education, health care, and housing standards in the territories. A court system was established, and the commissioner's advisory council

The RCMP used to patrol with dog teams, but for some years they have been motorized. There are police detachments in all the major settlements of the north.

Blubber and Fur

The explorers of the north found it was not a frozen waste. Its seas teemed with life and the forests south of the treeline held a fortune in fur. Hoping for profit rather than glory, fur traders and whaling men converged on the north and turned it to their advantage.

Fort Resolution, the first fur trading post on Great Slave Lake, had been established in 1786. Following Mackenzie's journey down his river, many more posts were built along its banks and in the hinterland. In one period, three separate companies were involved, but by 1821 the three had been amalgamated as the Hudson's Bay Company.

All through the forest, local Dene were induced to give up hunting big game and instead concentrate on trapping small furbearers. Gradually they came to depend on goods supplied by the traders, and left their families in camps at the trading posts while they attended to their traplines.

Meanwhile, whaling men were penetrating Davis Strait and Baffin Bay. British vessels were there in 1821, and ships from the United States followed.

Each winter, Inuit women made double suits of caribou fur for each member of the family. The outer skin was worn with the fur outside and was discarded in spring. The inner skin was worn with the fur next to the body, allowing air to circulate and keep the body dry.

Steam supplanted sail, and by the 1860s whalers were active in nearly all the navigable waters of the eastern arctic.

Often the whalers enlisted Inuit to hunt and trap for them. They returned to their homes with polar bear skins and other trophies besides their rich harvest of blubber and whalebone. As the industry grew, United States whalers sailed around Alaska to reach the western arctic and the Beaufort sea.

The whalers learned much from the Inuit, and taught them much too. The Inuit were introduced to wooden boats, firearms, foreign clothing, and new tools, as well as to luxuries like biscuits, tea, and tobacco. Like the Dene, many of the Inuit gave up hunting for their own needs and instead joined forces with the kabloonas.

By the end of the nineteenth century the whaling industry was in decline. As if to fill the breach, the Hudson's Bay Company opened its first stores in the far north. Other companies and individual traders followed suit, and in the 1920s many Inuit became comparatively wealthy through trapping arctic fox.

Fashions changed and the fox market collapsed. The Hudson's Bay Company once more absorbed its competition, and Inuit again hunted and trapped to stay alive. Only in recent years have fur prices advanced to the point where trapping can again make men rich.

was enlarged to include elected members. By the early 1960s there was talk of splitting the N.W.T. into two parts divided by the treeline.

The idea provoked an outcry, and the federal government appointed a commission to study its options. The commission reported in 1966, and recommended that the territories should remain a unit. They should be given their own capital and more say in their own affairs, and they should move towards provincial status.

The recommendations were accepted and Ottawa prepared to act. Yellowknife was selected as capital and a public service was recruited. Stuart Hodgson of British Columbia was appointed the territories' first resident commissioner, and September 1967 saw his arrival in Yellowknife as Ottawa surrendered some of its powers.

Dene gather at Fort Rae to celebrate Treaty Day. Under the N.W.T. treaties, each registered Indian may receive $5.00 per year from the federal government.

43

MINES AND MINERALS

Martin Frobisher's sponsors sank fortunes into mining fool's gold on Baffin Island, and Samuel Hearne endured years of hardship in his fruitless quest for native copper. In 1789 Alexander Mackenzie noticed oil seepages on the banks of the Mackenzie river, but ignored them.

Precious metals, base metals, petroleum — even the earliest white visitors spotted the N.W.T.'s mineral potential, though they did not profit from it. Their successors have been more fortunate. For some decades mining has been the territories' leading industry,

and since 1970 vast fields of petroleum have been revealed in the west and north.

Prospectors entered the territories at the time of the Yukon gold rush, but found little to interest them. One pair came to a bizarre end in the valley of the South Nahanni river, where their bodies were found minus their heads. Several promising base metals deposits were noticed, but there was no prospect of transporting ore south.

Instead, the first positive move came through petroleum exploration. A drilling crew explored the Mackenzie river and struck oil at Norman Wells, west of Great Bear Lake. Again, there was a

A towering headframe tops the principal shaft of Yellowknife's Con mine, one of Canada's leading producers of gold. In the distance are the city and Great Slave Lake.

transport problem. The crude oil was distilled on the spot to supply products for the area — fuel for heaters, electrical generators, and aircraft.

In the 1930s, prospectors once more entered the territories to search for metals. Pitchblende was found at the east end of Great Bear Lake, and radium and uranium were mined there until 1960. The uranium is exhausted, but the mine is still worked for silver. Two more precious metals mines are operating elsewhere on the lake.

Gold was found in the hard rock of Precambrian Shield around Great Slave Lake. Half a dozen mines were in operation before the outbreak of World War II. The goldfields have had a checkered career, but two large mines are still working on the outskirts of Yellowknife.

One of the first moves to develop the N.W.T.'s base metals came in 1955, when a nickel mine was established in Rankin Inlet, on the west coast of Hudson Bay. At the time there was no settlement there, but local Inuit were induced to give up trapping and work for wages. The mine closed down in 1962.

Winter and summer, drilling crews probe the sediments of the arctic in search of oil and natural gas. Some are based on arctic islands, some on artificial islands built for the purpose.

Two years later, a major lead-zinc mine was opened at Pine Point near Great Slave Lake's south shore. A railroad was built to transport Pine Point ore concentrate to the south, where it was smelted and refined at Trail in British Columbia. Pine Point has since become the world's largest lead-zinc surface mine.

Another major lead-zinc operation has gone into production at Nanisivik, in the far north of Baffin Island. As at Rankin Inlet, local Inuit have been recruited for the work force, together with many outsiders. Nanisivik is the most northerly mine in the world, and its ore concentrate is shipped out by bulk carriers during summer.

There is a tungsten mine in the Mackenzie mountains close to the Yukon boundary. Looking ahead, there are plans to open new lead-zinc mines at Cotwoito Lake in the heart of the barren lands and on Little Cornwallis Island in the middle of the arctic archipelago. There is a potential uranium mine near Baker Lake in Keewatin.

Mining companies looking for base metals concentrate on the hard rock of the Precambrian Shield, the eastern arctic, and the vast hinterland stretching west from Hudson Bay to the edge of the Mackenzie basin. That is where the sediments begin, the deep strata probed by petroleum companies seeking new deposits of oil and natural gas.

Flanked by the Shield and the Mackenzie mountains to the west, the sediments spill northwards down the valley of the Mackenzie and under the sea beyond. They surface again as the western islands of the arctic archipelago. Petroleum companies have had to develop revolutionary technology to discover the secrets they contain.

At first, the companies concentrated on the Mackenzie valley. Norman Wells were still in production, and even today they fulfill most of the energy needs of the western arctic. In the delta, drilling crews battled muskeg swamps to establish sturdy platforms for their rigs without damaging the delicate environment.

In the early 1960s several holes were drilled in the arctic archipelago, but without success. Then came the discovery of natural gas off Alaska's north coast in 1968. Soon petroleum companies were probing the territories'

coastal waters too, and made their first strike in 1970.

By 1973 there were 80 drilling rigs at work in various parts of the territories. Some crews operated on land, some from drilling ships, and some from artificial islands created in the Beaufort sea. The petroleum companies kept their results to themselves, but large regions of the north were explored and assessed.

At the time, it seemed certain that a pipeline would be built to carry natural gas southwards. It would be routed through the Mackenzie valley, and would carry not only the territories' production but also gas from Alaska. Then the Canadian government appointed a royal commission to study the impact of such a pipeline.

The commission consisted of a single man, Thomas Berger of Vancouver. Berger travelled to communities along the proposed route to sound out local opinion, and in 1977 presented his report. He recommended that to protect Dene and Inuit lifestyles, the pipeline

project should be postponed for at least ten years, and that for environmental reasons no pipeline should ever be constructed across the northern Yukon.

The recommendations made sense, and the petroleum companies had to think again. Some made plans to ship oil and natural gas from arctic locations by sea. In 1969, Canadian icebreakers had helped the tanker SS Manhattan of the United States to sail through the northwest passage in both directions.

As yet, no arctic wells have entered production, and there are no immediate plans to develop any. The Canadian government has passed strict environmental laws to protect the northern ecosystem, and has set rigid engineering standards for tankers that might sail in it. The N.W.T.'s petroleum potential is as bright as ever, but it will be some time before it can be exploited.

Twin drills attack the rockface down Pine Point lead-zinc mine, located near the south shore of Great Slave Lake.

FISH AND FUR

There was a time when the Inuit and Dene had no alternative but to live from the land. That has all changed, but few of them can resist the call of the wild. Many still hunt, trap, and fish professionally, and others join in whenever they have the time.

Land mammals in the territories are the concern of the N.W.T. wildlife service. Fishing and the hunting of sea mammals (not including polar bears) are controlled by federal authorities. 'Native' northerners — Inuit, Dene, Métis, and long-established kabloonas and their descendants — have special privileges under both jurisdictions.

To hunt land mammals, the native northerners must obtain a general hunting licence. With two notable exceptions, this allows them to hunt or trap unlimited numbers of any species, provided it is in season. The exceptions are polar bears and musk oxen, which are subject to strict annual quotas assigned not to individuals but to communities.

The polar bear and musk ox hunts affect only Inuit and a few kabloonas. Musk oxen are killed chiefly for their meat, but polar bears are in demand for their pelts. To make sure the polar bear quota is not exceeded, wildlife officers issue tags that must be attached to the pelts before they may be sold.

Another animal hunted for its meat is the caribou. Both Inuit and Dene used to rely on caribou to provide them with clothing, shelter, and much more besides, and each family took several score of them every year. Now they kill fewer, and caribou are popular with kabloona sportsmen who may take up to five in a season.

The Dene trap the furbearers of the boreal forest, particularly lynx, marten, and muskrat. In the ratting season each spring, whole families spread across the frozen Mackenzie delta to set snares by the muskrat 'push-ups' or lodges. When the ice breaks up, they continue the hunt from canoes, shooting muskrats in the water.

For the Inuit, the most valuable

Inuit still make skin kayaks for hunting and fishing, but today most are propelled by outboard motors rather than by paddle power.

furbearer is the arctic fox, but it is notoriously difficult to trap. Considerable skill must be used in concealing the trap so that the fox will not be suspicious. Trappers on Banks Island have mastered the art and are being recruited to give lessons in other parts of the north.

Native northerners do not need a licence to hunt sea mammals, but there are restrictions. Each hunter is limited to an annual catch of seven walrus, prized for their ivory tusks. As with polar bears, there is a quota system controlling the hunt for horned narwhals, and similar limits will be imposed to protect beluga whales.

As yet there are no restrictions on the seal hunt, which remains an Inuit specialty. In the old days Inuit spent hours poised motionless over holes concealed in the sea ice, waiting for a seal to come up for air. The seal betrayed its presence by nudging a bone placed across the hole, and the hunter struck home with a harpoon.

Sometimes a hunter waited beside a breathing hole for a whole day without success. Few modern Inuit would have such patience. Instead, they travel to open water on snowmobiles and hunt with high-powered rifles. They also use snowmobiles to hunt caribou, musk ox, and polar bears, and to work their traplines.

Each summer, many Inuit families fish for arctic char — members of the salmon family — as they return to rivers to spawn. Some man longliners equipped with gillnets, some are in open 'peterheads' — wooden boats like those that whalers used. The Inuit keep some of the fish for their own use, but many are sent to markets in the south.

Inland, there is a year-round commercial fishery in the western half of Great Slave Lake. Whitefish make up the bulk of the catch, which also includes lake trout and arctic grayling. In summer, the fish are caught by a fleet of 'whitefish boats,' each carrying four or five crew, and a number of two-man skiffs, all using gillnets. In winter, gillnets are strung beneath the ice.

Travel Arctic

Package tours to the north pole, backpacking on Baffin Island, a week at a fishing lodge, a raft trip on the Nahanni river — each year some 20 000 tourists converge on the N.W.T. and make powerful contributions to the economy.

Tourism has become the territories' third-largest industry after mining and trapping. The lion's share of the revenue goes to the fishing lodges, which tend to attract the well-to-do. Most of the lodges are on the east arm of Great Slave Lake and around Great Bear Lake, and all but one are accessible only by air.

The fishing lodges are open from June to September, and that is the season preferred by wilderness seekers too. The national parks are major attractions, even though Nahanni and Auyuittuq are difficult to reach. In many parts of the north, U-Paddle canoes can be hired from Hudson's Bay Company stores.

Some tourists team up with professional outfitters who act as their guides and their chaperones. Motorboats cruise the Mackenzie river, fishing longliners explore the fjords of Baffin Island, and processions of trailriders sample the Mackenzie mountains. In winter, an outfitter offers dog team expeditions in Wood Buffalo National Park.

As yet, few package tours visit the N.W.T., because communities outside Yellowknife are short of accommodation. However, many outsiders travel north to see the midnight sun at the summer solstice. Charter flights carry day trippers to Frobisher Bay from Toronto and Montreal and to Inuvik from cities of the west.

Tourists brave the racing waters of the Nahanni river, one of many offbeat vacation experiences offered in the Northwest Territories.

TRANSPORTATION

Soon after striking oil at Norman Wells in 1920, the company responsible bought two German-made cabin aircraft to transport employees to the north. The pilots agreed to make their first run well ahead of the Mackenzie river's spring break-up.

No aircraft had flown the route before, but fuel was cached at regular intervals. The pilots left Peace River in Alberta near the end of March 1921, and stopped at Fort Vermilion, Hay River, and Fort Providence before they reached Fort Simpson. There, one of the machines crash-landed and broke its propeller.

The other machine landed safely, but its engine seized. Its propeller was transferred to the first and the pilots prepared to take off. This time they ploughed into a deep drift and broke the second propeller. Fortunately, a local man volunteered to make a third, and did so using oak sleigh boards and moose-hoof glue.

Miraculously, the makeshift propeller carried the aircraft south again. Today it is displayed in Ottawa, a memorial to a generation of bush pilots who learned to fly by the seat of their pants. They navigated by the stars and the lie of the land, and had to rely on their own resourcefulness to keep themselves safe from trouble.

Modern northerners take aviation for granted. Most communities have their own airports or all-weather landing strips, and all but the smallest are linked by scheduled services. Aircraft ferry not only passengers but also freight of all kinds — sometimes food or fuel supplies, sometimes more exotic cargoes like furs or gold ingots.

Of course, most freight is carried by surface routes. Icebreakers escort the annual sea-lift convoys that supply communities in the eastern and central arctic during the short summer. Ships lie offshore while barges and landing-craft shuttle cargo to the beach, or deliberately run aground so that they can off-load into trucks when the tide goes out.

Most of the cargoes destined for the arctic come from Montreal. In Hudson Bay, communities are supplied by sea-lift barges from Churchill. Barges are also used on the Mackenzie river, where powerful tugs push up to four at a time to supply Inuvik and settlements on the way, and perhaps out into the Beaufort sea beyond.

The river is an efficient transport route, but it is open for navigation only four months of the year. Most of the river barges are loaded at Hay River, the head of the railroad that runs to Alberta. Besides general freight, the railroad carries lead-zinc concentrate from the mine at Pine Point.

Running parallel to the railroad is the N.W.T.'s only road link with South-

A research ship ploughs through light sea ice in the polar sea. Each summer, icebreakers escort convoys of supply ships to communities in the eastern and central arctic.

Aviation has conquered the territories' immense distances. Here, an RCMP patrol aircraft unloads supplies at Pangnirtung on Baffin Island.

Dogs and Snowmobiles

Architects have praised Inuit snow houses, efficiency experts have acclaimed their kayaks, and tailors have enthused about their caribou clothing. Many more of their inventions were masterpieces of economy and good sense, but the most remarkable was their use of dogs.

Introduced by the Thule people, the pure-bred Eskimo dog was large and white, and was probably descended from Siberian wolves. Dogs and sleds spread across the north from Alaska to Greenland, where white men learned how to use them. The kabloonas later introduced the idea to Indian country, and the snowshoe people quickly took advantage.

Reacting to local landforms, dog handlers developed several styles of harnessing their teams. Dene preferred the so-called Indian hitch, with dogs in single file between two parallel traces. Western Inuit used the Alaskan hitch with pairs of dogs attached to a single trace running down the middle of the team.

Inuit families park their snowmobiles while attending church. Even tiny communities have at least one church, whether Catholic or Protestant.

Inuit of the north and east used the fan hitch, each dog attached to the sled by its own trace and choosing its own path. The arrangement worked well on rugged terrain and out on sea ice. Even if some of the dogs fell into a crevasse, they would not take the rest of the team with them.

Inuit born before the 1960s grew up with working dog teams, but saw a revolution. Within a few years nearly the whole population turned from dogs to snowmobiles, realizing that the machines were swifter and more efficient. A few dogs were kept as pets, but most were slaughtered and no more teams were broken in.

In Dene country, many trappers prefer dog teams to snowmobiles, though there are fewer than there used to be. The dogs are small and wiry, quite different from the traditional dogs of the Inuit. Many whites train dog teams for sport and race them at Hay River, Yellowknife, and elsewhere.

Throughout the north, snowmobiles have become a way of life. Like dogs before them, they are used to haul canvas sleds that carry a drum of gasoline, a tool box, a food supply, and a sleeping bag. If they break down, there are few repairs that the drivers cannot make without help.

ern Canada. The Mackenzie highway approaches Hay River, then turns west towards Fort Simpson. Subsidiary highways connect with Yellowknife, Hay River, and other points, and in due course the Mackenzie highway may be extended to the delta.

Opened in 1979, the Dempster highway connects delta communities with the Yukon. Each winter a number of temporary roads are bulldozed through the snow, providing access to remote mining and exploration sites. In addition, northerners develop their own long-distance trails for snowmobiles and other tracked vehicles.

One serious shortcoming of the highway system is the lack of a bridge across the Mackenzie river. In summer there are ferries and in winter vehicles cross the ice, but during freeze-up and break-up Yellowknife is marooned. Freight must be flown in from Hay River or elsewhere, or airlifted across the river by helicopter.

On the Mackenzie river, powerful tugs push supply barges to communities from Great Slave Lake to the Beaufort sea and beyond.

LIVING STANDARDS

Even 30 years ago, most Inuit still lived in temporary camps, moving from location to location as the seasons changed. Possessions were kept to a minimum — skins for warmth and shelter,

Northerners tend to take aviation for granted. Here, a party of Inuit embark on a Canadian Coast Guard helicopter to be carried to a larger community.

cooking pots and implements, and the universal stone lamps used for heating and lighting.

Then the Inuit moved into permanent homes and gradually revised their old living styles. They bought and used furniture imported from the south — tables, chairs, beds, and dressers. Electricity and heating systems were installed, and the Inuit became used to novelties like doors and windows.

The transformation has been so

When travelling, Inuit like to make occasional stops for a warming cup of tea — a beverage introduced by whalers.

complete that many young Inuit have never known an alternative. The majority have never slept a night in a snow house and have never so much as seen a working dog team. They have grown up in a world of snowmobiles and aircraft, telephones and television, stoves, hair dryers, and refrigerators.

Today, most Inuit settlements rely on wage economies revolving around their trading stores. Many have two — one a Hudson's Bay Company post, the other a co-operative in which local people hold shares. The stores stock groceries, clothing, furniture, appliances, and souvenirs for occasional tourists.

Besides the trading stores, most communities hold at least one church, a school, a post office, and perhaps a nursing station. The N.W.T. government is represented, and there is a community office and probably a recreation hall. There may be a curling rink, and one of the most popular facilities will be the school gymnasium.

Like the Inuit, the Dene have abandoned the nomadic patterns of their past and all now live in permanent settlements. Superficially their communities look the same as the Inuit's, except that they are surrounded by trees and they may include high teepees to smoke fish and provide extra storage.

Both above and below the treeline, communities hold large populations of pet dogs tied up outside their owners' doors. Snowmobiles roar down local trails, and at least in Inuit settlements there are many more snowmobiles than trucks and cars. Many families expect to buy a new snowmobile every year.

Dene communities look to their chief for leadership, though increasingly the important decisions are being made by elected settlement councils. Inuit have no tradition of chieftaincy, though there used to be an unofficial hierarchy determined by men's prowess as hunters. Today, speaking skills are more important.

All the N.W.T.'s permanent communities have a white population, however small. Missionaries, traders, nurses, teachers, police, and welfare officers are active all through the territories. Most see themselves as only temporary, but some of the missionaries have spent a lifetime in the north and expect to die there.

The more radical Dene are wary of white men, regarding them as representatives of a colonial power that has taken away their freedom. Inuit, on the other hand, welcome kalbloonas' help, but look forward to a time in the near future when they can take control of their own affairs.

The Outposts

Not all Dene and Inuit are impressed with modern settlements. Many prefer to live close to nature as in the old days. To help them return to the land, in 1975 the N.W.T. government introduced the Outpost program for families prepared to move to the wilds.

The families undertook to live off the land for all or part of the year. The government gave them travelling money, a grubstake towards the first year's supplies, and a grant towards some form of shelter — probably a cabin. Above the treeline, Outpost families also received a grant towards the cost of fuel oil.

By 1979, nearly 50 groups were taking part. Some outposts consisted of a single family, but the largest contained 60 people. Outpost children could not attend school and there was little health care, but the government felt that the benefits of wilderness living greatly outweighed the disadvantages.

Even apart from the Outpost program, many Dene and Inuit return to nature for extended periods of the year. On the Mackenzie delta, whole families of the Dene take part in the ratting season between March and June. On Hudson Bay and in the arctic, Inuit families camp near the sea for the fishing season.

Some Inuit like to spend weekends in the wilderness, hunting and trapping

Enjoying the mild temperatures of mid-summer, an Outpost family dries sealskins at its camp close to the sea.

and perhaps sleeping in a snow house. Many younger Inuit grew up with little idea of how to build the famous shelters, but the old skills are being revived. Igloo building contests have become a part of local celebrations.

To build a snow house, the Inuit first outline its shape in the snow. Using a snow knife or snow saw, they cut large, rectangular blocks and bevel their edges to give them a slight lean. The base blocks are trimmed to a wedge shape, and the Inuit add successive blocks in a spiral until the last ones seal the roof.

Igloo building usually requires at least two people. One cuts the blocks and hands them to his partner, who remains inside the snow house until the last one is in place. He then cuts an opening at floor level, and adds an entrance porch outside. Finally, the walls are chinked to fill gaps between blocks, and smoothed to look neat.

In the past, Inuit built large complexes of interconnected snow houses, one for each family. Today igloos are more modest, and Inuit furnish them with sleeping bags rather than the caribou rugs of old. Few Inuit have any ambition to go back to snow houses permanently, but they are proud to share in the traditions of their ancestors.

A vote in progress at the N.W.T.'s legislative council, which sits in a Yellowknife hotel. The council meets for three sessions each year.

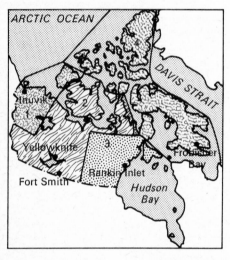

For ease of administration, the Northwest Territories are divided into four regions, each with its own regional headquarters. The regions are: 1. Inuvik (headquarters Inuvik); 2. Fort Smith (headquarters Fort Smith); 3. Keewatin (headquarters Rankin Inlet); and 4. Baffin Island (headquarters Frobisher Bay).

THE ADMINISTRATION

For the rest of the country, 1967 was the year of Canada's centennial. For the N.W.T. it was also the year power was transferred from Ottawa to Yellowknife. The territories' embryo public service arrived by air on September 13.

At the time, the territories were being administered by the federal Department of Indian Affairs and Northern Development. They were organized as two districts separated by the 102nd west meridian, Mackenzie and the eastern arctic. At first the new public service was to have full authority only in Mackenzie.

As the territorial administration found its feet, the federal government entrusted it with fresh responsibilities. Some were social, like housing; some cultural, like education; some economic, like business development. The one major responsibility reserved to the federal government was control of natural resources apart from wildlife.

In 1970 the federal administration was made responsible for the eastern arctic as well as Mackenzie. The public service was expanding rapidly, mainly through federal transfers, and so were its programs. To make sure that no parts of the territories were neglected, Yellowknife redivided them into four regions, each with an administrative headquarters.

Under the new system, general policies and programs were developed in Yellowknife, and each region organized its local programs. Each department of the administration was represented in the regional headquarters — Frobisher Bay in Baffin, Rankin Inlet in Keewatin, Inuvik for the delta, and Fort Smith for the western area.

The various territorial departments are headed by members of an executive committee. This committee is chaired by the commissioner, and includes his two senior assistants and three members representing the territorial council. Like the Yukon's executive committee, the N.W.T.'s sets the policies followed by the administration.

These policies are regularly debated in the territorial council, which meets for three sessions each year, usually in the banqueting room of a Yellowknife hotel. The commissioner and his deputy are not members of the council but can be heard as witnesses. The council's deliberations are controlled by an elected speaker.

As yet there are no political parties in the territorial council, but even so debates are lively. The federal government pegs the number of members between 15 and 25 at the council's discretion. The three members selected to serve on the executive committee answer to the council like cabinet ministers.

In theory the council's decisions are subject to Ottawa's disallowance, but in practice Ottawa does not interfere. However, the council is not allowed to introduce money bills granting funds to the administration, so Ottawa controls the pursestrings. On the other hand, the council can refuse to sanction the administration's budget proposals.

One side of government in the north

In recent years both the Dene and the Inuit have become politically conscious. This is a Dene meeting called to discuss land claims.

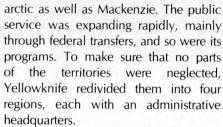

is quite separate from the others. The judiciary came into being in 1955, when Jack Sissons was appointed the territories' first judge. Before his arrival, northerners on trial had been taken to courts in Southern Canada, but Sissons aimed to carry justice 'to every man's door.'

In the years that followed, Sissons flew tens of thousands of kilometres each year as he ranged across the north. Courts were held in schoolhouses, community halls, and even aboard a moored floatplane. Local jurors were sworn in, and in many communities the whole population turned out for the hearing.

Today, the Supreme Court of the Northwest Territories still has only one judge, though deputy judges from Southern Canada are brought in as needed. The Supreme Court is housed in modern quarters in Yellowknife, and periodically sits in courthouses that have been built in Hay River, Fort Smith, Inuvik, and Frobisher Bay.

The courthouses also serve the territorial court, where a judge appointed by the territory hears less serious cases. Most of the N.W.T.'s court work, however, is handled by part-time justices of the peace who sit in their own communities. The JPs include many Dene and Inuit, and the bulk of their work is deciding minor cases like liquor offences and traffic violations.

The Interpreters

For more than half of the N.W.T.'s population, English is at best a second language. Many older Inuit speak only Inuktitut, and the Dene groups speak versions of four distinct languages that are no closer to one another than French is to Italian.

The Inuit are proud of their language, and some feel it is more efficient than English. Certainly it is more precise. Where a single English word may cover a range of meanings, Inuktitut supplies separate words that express the subtle differences. Besides, Inuktitut can combine several ideas to build a single long word with the exact meaning required.

In the past, groups of Inuit were isolated from one another and spoke dialects that other Inuit found difficult to understand. Now, an Inuit language commission has studied the problem and is defining a standard form of Inuktitut. The commission has been considering not only the spoken word but the written word too.

In many schools, Inuktitut is being used as the language of instruction in the first three grades and is being taught as a subject later on. Inuit interpreters are on hand in hospitals and courts, and provide simultaneous translations at meetings of the territorial council and other bodies. Official documents are translated too.

Through measures like these, the federal and territorial governments have conferred special status on Inuktitut. The language has been gaining strength, even though few Inuit in the western arctic want to use it. Those who do are encouraged by frequent Inuktitut broadcasts over the CBC's northern service.

In serving the Dene, the governments have run into problems. The many languages and dialects make it impossible to provide an adequate interpreter service. Some dialects have never been written down, and others are expressed in a syllabic script that has too few symbols to express all their vowels and consonants.

Of the four Dene languages, only Dogrib is exclusive to the N.W.T. Chipewyan is spoken in northern Saskatchewan and Manitoba. Versions of Slavey are heard in northern British Columbia and Alberta, and are used by the Hares as well as by the Slaveys proper. The Loucheux spoken in the mountains is shared by Indians of the Yukon.

Inuktitut is almost an official language in the N.W.T. At meetings of the legislative council and elsewhere, a corps of government interpreters provides simultaneous translations between Inuktitut and English.

ᐃᓄᐃᑦ ᓄᓇᒥ ᑲᓇᑕᒥ 70-ᒥᑦ

ᐃᓯᒪᓯᐅᐅᓄᑉ ᐸᑦ ᐃᓄᐃᑦ ᓄᓇᒥᓂ ᐱᕇᑦᐊᑎᑕᐅᔭ ᑕᑯᒪᓪ ᓇᓄᑲᐅᕐᑕ -ᐊᕐᓂᒃ, ᓇᒍᐊᑕᐅᕐᓇᐊᕐᓯᓂ -ᒪᔪ ᐅᑲᓄᐱᑎᓂ ᒪᐅᕐᓂ ᐊᒪ ᐃᓄᐃᑦ ᓄᓇᓕᑦ ᐱᕇᓇᕐᒪᓕ ᐱᕇ-ᓇᐊᑎᒍ ᐊᒪ ᑕᒪᐱᕈ ᑕᐅ-ᐊᕇᐊᔪᓂ ᑲᓇᑎᑲᐊᕐᓂᓗ ᑕᐅ-ᐅᑲᑕᓕ ᑲᓇᑦᒦᐅᑲᐊᓗ ᐊᒪ ᑲ -ᓇᑦᒦᐅᑕ ᐊᕇᕐᓂᒃ. ᑲᓇᑦᒦᐅᑕ ᐅᐊᐸᕐᖃᑐᑦ ᐊᕇᖃᓇᒃ ᑲᓇ ᐱᑎ-ᖃᓇᐊᒪᓕ ᓄᓇᓄᑦ ᒦᓇᐅ ᐊᒪ ᑲ -ᓇᐱᕇᐊᑉᑎᒪ ᐃᓄᐃᑦ ᓄᓇᓂ ᐊ -ᒪᔪ ᑕᑯᐊᑕ ᐃᓄᐊ ᐊᒍᕐᓯ ᓯᕐᓂ-ᓂᕐᓂᒃ. ᐊᒍᕇ, ᐊᐊᕐᒪᐊᒃ ᐊᒪ ᑕᑎᑲᐅᐊᑦ ᐊᑭᐊᓂ ᐃᑕᓄᐅᑲᕐᒦ ᐃᑲᕈᑎ ᐱᑎᒪᓵᓂ ᓄᓇᕐᐊ ᐃᓄᐊ ᓄᓇᕐᐊᑯᑎᓕᓂ ᐊᖃ ᔪᑎᕇᐊᒪᕇᐊ-ᓗᒦ.

Missionaries in the western arctic taught Inuit to read and write in Roman characters. Those in the eastern arctic adapted a syllabic script originally devised for Cree Indians. An Inuktitut language commission has been trying to reconcile the two systems.

TOWNS AND HAMLETS

Besides the capital, there are more than 60 permanent communities in the N.W.T. A few qualify as towns or villages, but the great majority are small and are classified as hamlets or unincorporated settlements.

After Yellowknife, the largest of the communities is Hay River across Great Slave Lake, the terminus of the railroad from the south. There, cargoes for the delta are loaded aboard Mackenzie river barges, and commercial fishing boats enter the harbour with their catches of whitefish and lake trout.

A rail spur and a highway connect Hay River with Pine Point, the mining town to the east. Another highway crosses Wood Buffalo National Park to reach Fort Smith, the home of the N.W.T.'s adult vocational training centre. Fort Smith is situated on the Slave river, the waterway that connects Great Slave Lake with Lake Athabasca.

Hay River, Fort Smith, and indeed most of the N.W.T.'s communities were founded to serve the fur trade. Fort Resolution at the mouth of the Slave river had its start in 1786, and so did Fort Providence near the start of the Mackenzie river. In both cases the present settlement is some way from the post's original site.

Fort Simpson down the Mackenzie was founded in 1804, and is the oldest post that has been in continuous use. Fort Good Hope on the lower Mackenzie came into being in 1805, Fort Liard in the south-west in 1807, and Fort Norman on the middle Mackenzie in 1810. Many other posts were founded in the region but were abandoned long ago.

River convoys link these lonely communities as they did at the height of the fur trade. They serve Norman Wells too, and barges are diverted to Fort Franklin on Great Bear Lake. Most barges are carried on to the delta, particularly to Inuvik, which is the third-largest community in the N.W.T.

Inuvik is a modern creation, hewn from the bush in 1955 after serious flooding wrought havoc in Aklavic. Not all of Aklavik's residents were prepared to move, so now there are twin communities, the old and the new. To the north is Tuktoyaktuk on the coast, a

The Capital

In the 1930s, Yellowknife was no more than a tent-frame mining camp, perched on a rocky peninsula in Great Slave Lake. Today it is a bustling city with a population of nearly 10 000, a mining town, seat of government, and commercial and social capital all in one.

Yellowknife's 'Old Town' is quieter than in the time of the pioneers. Its old gambling houses have gone, and so has Glamour Alley and its ladies of the night. Even so, the buildings that remain still hug the sides of a huge central rock, now topped by a striking memorial to the bush pilots who opened the north.

Bush flying operations still crowd Old Town, their aircraft using the lake as a runway. Small industries abound there as well, together with cunningly designed new homes that make the most of the spectacular views. Old Town and Latham Island near by have become industrial and residential suburbs of the New Town built on higher ground inland.

New Town was surveyed in 1945 and gradually occupied from that year on. There was a spurt forward in 1960 when Yellowknife was linked with the Mackenzie highway, and another in 1967 when scores of public servants arrived. In 1970 the capital was incorporated as a city, and it has expanded steadily ever since.

Yellowknifers turn out in force for the annual Caribou Carnival. A popular event is the dog pull, when animals strain to haul sleds piled with sandbags.

In spite of highrise apartment blocks and modern shopping centres, Yellowknife is still a frontier town at heart. Dene and Inuit arrive from all over the territories, and few of the white residents were born there. One result is a high level of racial tolerance that sets an example for cities in Southern Canada.

Yellowknifers believe in an active social life, and sporting events are varied and frequent. One of the most bizarre is a midnight golf tournament, taking advantage of mid-summer's perpetual daylight. In March, Yellowknifers celebrate the Caribou Carnival, a week-long festival that features gruelling dog and snowmobile races on Great Slave Lake, and many other contests open to all comers.

Populations

Statistics Canada's mini-census of 1976 showed that the Northwest Territories had a total population of 42 609. The largest communities had populations as follows:

Yellowknife	8256
Hay River	3268
Inuvik	3116
Frobisher Bay	2320

permanent settlement since 1934.

The delta region is one of the most stimulating in the N.W.T., a meeting place where Dene, Inuit, and kabloonas are in close contact and adopt one another's cultures. During the 1960s and 1970s, Inuvik became rich, while petroleum companies explored the delta, the arctic islands, and the sea in between.

East of the delta, the treeline dips sharply south. Above it is Inuit country, with a thin scattering of settlements on the coasts of the mainland and the islands offshore. In spite of their tiny size, many of them are known to people all over the world because of the success of their arts and crafts.

Holman on Victoria Island, Gjoa Haven on King William Island, Pangnirtung on Baffin Island — like communities in the Mackenzie valley, most Inuit settlements grew up around fur trading posts and missions. Some were preceded by whaling bases, and a few were developed to serve the world outside.

country was at Chesterfield Inlet on the Keewatin coast, founded in 1912 with a Roman Catholic mission close by. Cape Dorset's was established in the following year. Baker Lake, the only settlement in the barrens, dates from 1916, and so

does Coppermine on Coronation Gulf.

Frobisher Bay, now regional headquarters of the eastern arctic, was founded as an air force base during World War II. In the 1950s it became the chief supply centre for construction of defence installations across the north. Rankin Inlet, headquarters for Keewatin, grew up around a nickel mine that survived for only seven years.

Another mining town, Nanisivik on northern Baffin Island, is the newest community in the arctic, but not the most northerly. That honour belongs to

Cheerful youngsters at Cape Dorset on Baffin Island, world-famous for its arts and crafts.

Grise Fjord on Ellesmere Island. It was settled by Inuit transplanted from northern Quebec and Pond Inlet on Baffin Island to strengthen Canada's presence near the top of the world.

Rae and its sister community Edzo comprise the N.W.T.'s largest community of Dene. The hamlets are located on the north arm of Great Slave Lake, north-west of the capital.

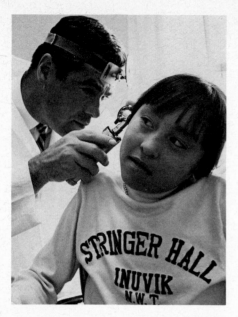

N.W.T. students receive regular medical checkups, as here in Inuvik on the Mackenzie delta.

HEALTH CARE

Before white men reached the north, the Dene and Inuit cured sickness by resorting to ancient folk remedies passed down from generation to generation. When the remedies did not work, they turned to a shaman or medicine man, part doctor and part priest.

The shamans claimed mystical powers, and even today some older Inuit believe in them. However, they steadily lost influence as people came to trust white man's medicine. All Hudson's Bay posts were equipped with a medicine chest, and RCMP patrols carried serious cases to a place where they could be treated.

Starting in 1867, a number of mission hospitals were built. Some of them survive today, but since 1954 health care has been a government responsibility. That was when the federal government set up a northern health service, serving both the N.W.T. and the Yukon and with its headquarters in Edmonton.

The immense distances in the N.W.T. make it costly to transport patients from one centre to another, and where feasible they are treated on the spot. Even tiny communities have their own 'health station' run by a lay dispenser who in most cases can contact a doctor or nurse by telephone.

The health station can provide basic first aid and medicine. The 'nursing station' found in communities of some size is more sophisticated. Staffed by professional nurses and regularly visited by physicians, it can provide emergency treatment, community health services, and baby clinics.

Groups of nursing and health stations are served by a system of 'regional hospitals,' where there are doctors in attendance. There are regional hospitals in Hay River, Inuvik, and Frobisher Bay, and one is to be built to serve the central arctic. They are staffed by general practitioners and perhaps by surgeons too.

Cases too serious for the regional hospitals are referred to the Stanton Yellowknife hospital in the capital, which is being expanded. More specialists are being added to its staff, and the hospital aims to provide treatment for patients who in the past would have been sent to hospitals in Southern Canada.

They are several advantages in treating such patients locally. Interpreters are available for those who do not speak English, and special food is served. Besides, in the past many of those sent south feared they would never return alive, whereas Yellowknife seems relatively close to home.

Step by step, the responsibility for health care in the N.W.T. is being transferred to the territorial government. For some years the government has operated health insurance and medicare schemes like those of Southern Canada. Now it is taking control of hospital administration too.

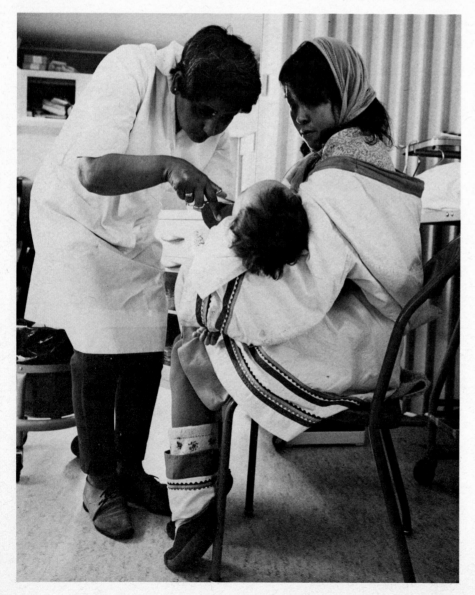

At the Pond Inlet nursing station on Baffin Island, a registered nurse attends to an Inuit mother and her baby.

The Schools

As early as 1867, the Roman Catholic mission at Fort Providence on the Mackenzie river opened a residential school. It was the forerunner of many such schools in remote communities across the north.

The mission schools catering to Dene were mainly Roman Catholic, while most of those for Inuit were Anglican. The missionaries taught their students to read, write, and think in English or perhaps French, and in the process tended to submerge local values in those of the world outside.

The steady erosion continued until World War II, when the federal government stepped in. Gradually mission schools were taken over or replaced, and education was made available throughout the N.W.T. In 1969 control of education was transferred to the territorial government.

Today, there are more than 60 schools in the N.W.T. Five are high schools located in Yellowknife, Hay River, Fort Smith, Inuvik, and Frobisher Bay. Each follows a version of Alberta's curriculum and some run hostels for students from out of town. The remainder are local public schools following the N.W.T.'s own curriculum.

Most of the teachers in the N.W.T.'s school system are from

Southern Canada and have limited experience of the north. To counterbalance their influence, the territorial government encourages communities to elect school committees that are empowered to hire staff, allot funds, and decide on local policy.

There are no post-secondary institutions in the N.W.T., but grants are provided for students wanting to attend college or university in the south. Besides, many northerners attend the adult vocational training centre at Fort

A typing class at the N.W.T.'s adult vocational training centre in Fort Smith near the Alberta boundary.

Smith, which offers courses in commerce, machine handling, and many other fields. Another school in Fort Smith trains Dene and Inuit as teachers and teaching assistants.

Many Dene and Inuit start school with no knowledge of English and are encouraged to take pride in their language. Here, a group of Inuit learn about the calendar.

Cape Dorset prints have become a byword in the international arts community. Local artists submit drawings and paintings, which, if accepted, are engraved in stone and printed in a limited edition as part of an annual collection.

ARTS AND CRAFTS

Inuktitut has no word for art, but it does have a word meaning 'making something the very best you can.' Until quite recent times, the Inuit had to create all their possessions for themselves, and took pains to make them beautiful as well as functional.

Inuit women were first-rate tailors, every year fashioning double suits of caribou hide for each member of the family, and probably sealskin boots to go with them. The men were ingenious carpenters in a land where wood was precious, and they used bone and walrus ivory to make hunting equipment and soapstone to make lamps and pots.

During winter, men often carved small objects from bone, stone, or ivory.

Some of them had spiritual significance. Others they made for fun, for instance toys for their children or toggles for their parkas. Coastal Inuit made simple souvenirs that found a market among visiting kabloonas.

That was the position until the early 1950s, when the painter James Houston was appointed administrator of West Baffin Island. Earlier, Houston had travelled in northern Quebec and Keewatin, buying up Inuit carvings that were later sold in Southern Canada. Now the federal government wanted him to encourage a crafts industry.

At the time, Ottawa was seriously concerned by the steady decline of caribou and other game species. Overhunting was to blame, and the Inuit needed new sources of income. On Houston's suggestion, Inuit carvers began producing large works in soapstone that would appeal to buyers in the south.

Success came early. Virtually everything the carvers produced was soon sold, and prices crept upwards. As years passed the carvings became popular in the United States and Europe as well as in Canada, and the best were accepted as high art. Individual carvers became famous.

Styles varied greatly from region to region and from carver to carver. Some pieces were loyal to nature in every detail. Some were near-abstract, a collage of many ideas. All reflected aspects of deep-rooted Inuit traditions — myths, legends, animals, and the experiences of everyday life.

Ironically, the Inuit themselves placed no great value on what they were doing. They appreciated the money it earned, but most preferred more manly occupations like hunting or fishing. Most of the notable carvers were

Most N.W.T. communities have developed an artistic specialty. Rankin Inlet's is wall hangings, part-patched and part-embroidered, and most of them marketed through a government agency.

old or handicapped, and even they refused to carve in summer when they could be out on the land.

As in the old days, nearly all the carvers were men. For women, James Houston introduced a new art form that he had studied in Japan — print-making on rice paper. First at Cape Dorset and later at other communities, women were encouraged to draw and paint scenes that could be engraved in stone.

Again, the results were spectacular. Each year, community co-operatives published series of prints that were as distinctive as the carvings. Soon individual artists became even better known than the carvers, and hamlets like Baker Lake, Pond Inlet on Baffin Island, and Holman on Victoria Island became world famous.

Today, print-making is an important industry in many of these settlements. The artists work on a freelance basis, but the technicians who make the prints are employed full-time. Like the carvers, the artists tend to recall the past rather than reflect the present, and insist that their work is valuable in reminding Inuit who they are.

Other art forms have been tried with varying success. Some communities produce ceramics, woven goods, or batiks. Several specialize in northern clothing, and the women of Rankin Inlet make patched wall hangings. Again, the work of notable individuals has become known far beyond Canada's borders.

In spite of all this activity, some serious collectors of Inuit art complain that overall standards have dropped. One reason may be that the artists now feel far removed from the lifestyle they are depicting. More and more, younger artists are turning to contemporary themes.

The most notable of these younger artists is Germaine Arnaktauyok, originally from Igloolik and now of Yellowknife. Significantly, her work is ad-

mired by the Inuit as much as by kabloonas, for it reflects the transition from the ancient to the modern, and has meaning for all.

Another notable painter of the north is Don Cardinal, a Métis from Alberta who now lives in Hay River. Cardinal uses ink and acrylics to capture the moods of the northern forests and of the people who live there, and is especially

sensitive to the world of the Dene who live around him.

The Dene have skills of their own. Their beadwork and embroidery is some of the brightest in Canada, and their moccasins and mukluks are much admired. So are their winter jackets, fringed in buckskin, and the weaving and moosehair tufting that are much in demand in Southern Canada.

NORTHERN GAMES

Every second year, the N.W.T. competes against the Yukon and Alaska at the Arctic Winter Games, a festival of northern sport. First held in 1970, the games are built around 15 events, three of them deliberately northern and the others universal.

The universal events vary from games to games, but always include basketball, cross-country skiing, curling, shooting, volleyball, and wrestling. The northern events are snowshow racing, snowshoe biathlon (shooting at targets placed at intervals along a cross-country course), and traditional Inuit games.

The Dene and Inuit had sports of their own long before white men arrived in the north. The Inuit favoured games of strength and agility. The Dene were fond of wrestling and long-distance running, on foot or on snowshoes. For fun, whole villages played forms of soccer or handball with a blown-up bladder or a skin stuffed with moss.

The Inuit sports chosen for the arctic games include the one-foot high kick, in which competitors leap high to reach a 'seal' suspended from a string, and must take off and land on the same foot. Another is the one-arm reach, when the athlete supports his whole body weight on one hand while reaching for the seal with the other.

The Arctic Winter Games feature only a tiny sample of the wide range of sports known to the Inuit. More are seen at the N.W.T.'s Northern Games, held in years when there are no arctic games. There, Inuit display their agility in such events as blanket-tossing (not unlike a trampoline competition) and gymnastics on a tightrope.

Among themselves, Inuit also enjoy tests of strength like pulling contests in which opponents loop twine around their ears or hook fingers in each others' mouths. All these competitions reflect the special qualities needed to survive in the north, among them strength, flexibility, endurance, and ability to stand pain.

Today, many of the Inuit games are being encouraged in northern schools, particularly those on the delta. Not only Inuit, but also Dene and kabloonas are taking part. Reciprocating, Inuit have become interested in 'southern' sports like volleyball, curling, and above all, gymnastics, which have much in common with their traditional sports.

One special success in the N.W.T. has been a coaching program initiated by a French missionary, Father Jean-

Blanket tossing, a sport long popular in the western arctic. Contestants use the blanket like a trampoline, and are awarded points for endurance and originality.

At the Arctic Winter Games, N.W.T. basketball players take on the team from the Yukon.

Special Events

Inuvik celebrates Delta Daze, Frobisher Bay has Toonik Tyme, and Hay River offers the Ookpik Carnival. All over the territories, communities organize local festivals to test the skills and strengths of everyone who wants to take part.

Some festivals are held with snow on the ground, some at the height of summer. They range from modest 'hamlet days' on the Keewatin coast to Yellowknife's Caribou Carnival which lasts for a week. Most combine sporting events with a beauty contest and perhaps a parade and a bonfire.

Dog races at Wrigley's Moccasin Carnival, muskrat skinning at Fort Smith's Wood Buffalo Frolics, snowmobile sprints at Sachs Harbour's White Fox Jamboree — events at the festivals are typical of the north. Many communities organize 'good woman' contests, in which competitors show off skills like baking bannock or skinning seals.

After a day's sport, many of the festivals end with a dance. In earlier days, both Dene and Inuit danced to drums, but interest in the old styles has waned. Instead, Dene like to jig to fiddle music, and Inuit square dance to an accordion in a style introduced by whaling men during the nineteenth century.

Most events at the festivals are open to all comers, but some have special status. The Caribou Carnival includes the Canadian championship dog derby, and Hay River's fall fair is

At a local sports day organized by a hamlet, Inuit women race to skin seals. Some hamlets organize a 'good woman' contest in which competitors show their prowess in a number of events.

built around the world championship fiddling and jigging contest. Even more remarkable are the world's most northerly golf tournament and regatta. Both are held at Tuktoyaktuk, though at different times of the year.

Marie Mouchet, whose 'parish' covered the delta and the northern Yukon too. Mouchet was an experienced cross-country skier, and believed that the sport would be perfect for the north, as it concentrated on the individual.

In the mid-1960s, Mouchet persuaded the federal government to fund a ten-year experiment in training Dene to ski. He concentrated on students attending the residential school in Inuvik, and the efforts soon bore fruit. Five of Mouchet's protégés were among Canada's eight cross-country skiers at the Sapporo Olympics of 1972.

The ten-year experiment is over, and the Inuvik group has dispersed. What survives is a conviction among Canada's northerners that they can hold their own against the world's top competitors, not only in their own events but in sports that have been introduced to the north well within living memory.

The one-foot high kick, a traditional Inuit sport that requires considerable agility. The competitor must kick a 'seal' suspended from a string, and must take off and land on the same foot.

INUKSHUIT

To the Inuit, an inukshuk is a 'thing that looks like a man.' It is the term they use for the hundreds of stone pillars that dot the northern landscape, slabs of rock piled one on another and in some cases reaching a height of three metres. Today's Inuit have adopted the inukshuit as symbols of their culture, a link with the spirits of their ancestors.

According to archaeologists, the first inukshuit may have been built earlier than 1000 A.D., perhaps by the Dorset people. Most, however, date from Thule times, erected between 1200 and the beginning of the eighteenth century. Some were constructed even more recently, in several cases by white explorers.

Different inukshuit had different functions. Many were intended as landmarks and direction finders in a land that was otherwise featureless. In some cases, inukshuit were built at intervals along a trail, helping winter travellers to find their way even when visibility was poor.

In some areas, Inuit used inukshuit to help them hunt caribou. A row of inukshuit was built near a watercourse, and hunters chased the caribou towards them. The caribou mistook the inukshuit for more hunters and took to the water, where the hunters could pursue them in their kayaks.

Elsewhere, two rows of inukshuit might be built in a funnel shape. One group of Inuit stampeded caribou into the funnel, and others lay in wait for them with bows and arrows. Often these killing sites had sacred significance, and parts of dead caribou were laid beside the inukshuit to appease the spirits.

Areas like northern Keewatin hold rock monuments of a different kind, known as *etigaseemante* or 'things that are raised from the ground.' Some are small and some are huge, but nearly all consist of a large flat rock set on several small ones, like an altar. They are at least 1000 years old, and even Inuit have no idea what they were for.

A lonely inukshuk near Frobisher Bay on Baffin Island, a stone beacon to guide travellers across the treeless barren lands of the north.

Photograph Credits

Canada Dept. of Indian Affairs and Northern Development: p. 7 bottom, p. 18 top and bottom, p. 30 top, p. 43 bottom; *Humphry Clinker*: p. 23 top and bottom, p. 24 top, p. 54, p. 58 bottom, p. 59 bottom, p. 61 bottom; *Cominco Ltd. Photo*: p. 44 top, p. 45; *Cyprus Anvil*: p. 26 bottom; *Government of the Northwest Territories Information Branch*: p. 32 top and bottom, p. 33, p. 38 bottom, p. 42, p. 43 top, p. 46, p. 48 top, p. 49 top and bottom, p. 50 top and bottom, p. 51, p. 52 top and bottom, p. 53, p. 55 top and bottom, p. 57 top and bottom, p. 58 top, p. 59 top, p. 60 top and bottom, p. 61 top; *Government of Yukon*: p. 4 top and bottom, p. 5 top and bottom, p. 16 top and bottom, p. 17 bottom, p. 20 top and bottom, p. 21, p. 22, p. 24 bottom, p. 25 bottom, p. 27 top, p. 29 bottom; *Gulf Oil*: p. 44 bottom; *John Hatch*: p. 14 top, p. 19 top and bottom; *Health and Welfare Canada*: p. 25 top, p. 56 top and bottom; *NWT Wildlife Service*: (George Calif) p. 3, p. 39 bottom; *Parks Canada*: p. 10 top and bottom, p. 27 bottom, p. 28, p. 30 bottom, (L. Freese) p. 31 top, p. 31 bottom, p. 34 top and bottom, p. 35 top and bottom, p. 47 top and bottom; *Barbara Preston*: p. 17 top; *Jim Robb*: p. 29 top; *Royal Canadian Mounted Police*: p. 48 bottom; *John Steeves*: p. 26 top; *Walter Weiss*: p. 62; *White Pass and Yukon Route*: p. 14 bottom, p. 15 top and bottom.

Acknowledgments

Many individuals, corporations, institutions, and government departments assisted us in gathering information and illustrations. Among them we owe special thanks to the following:

Germaine Arnaktauyok
Yves Assiniwi
Lavinia Brown
Chris Brunning
Canada Department of Health and Welfare
Canada Department of Indian Affairs and Northern
  Development
Council for Yukon Indians
Roland Courtemanche
Julie Cruikshank
Mike van Duffelen
Dene Nation
John Ferbey
Fisheries Canada

Ross Harvey
John Hatch
Hudson's Bay Company
North
Northern Electric Power Commission
N.W.T. Department of Education
N.W.T. Department of Health
N.W.T. Department of Information
N.W.T. Wildlife Service
Dwight and Judy Noseworthy
Edo Nyland
Parks Canada
Public Archives Canada
Barry Redfern

Athol Retallack
Jim Robb
Dennis Senger
Travel Arctic
White Pass and Yukon Route
Yukon Archives
Yukon Department of Education
Yukon Department of Information
Yukon Department of Tourism
Yukon Department of Transportation
Yukon Health Services
Yukon Legislative Council

If we have unwittingly infringed copyright in any photograph reproduced in this publication, we tender our sincere apologies and will be glad of the opportunity, upon being satisfied as to the owner's title, to pay an appropriate fee as if we had been able to obtain prior permission.

Canadian Cataloguing in Publication Data

Hocking, Anthony, 1944-
  The Yukon and Northwest Territories

(Canada series)

Includes index.
ISBN 0-07-082694-3

1. Yukon Territory. 2. Northwest Territories.
3. Yukon Territory — Description and travel.
4. Northwest Territories — Description and
travel. I. Title. II. Series.

FC4011.6.H63   971.9   C77-001610-3
F1091.H63

1 2 3 4 5 6 7 8 9 10 BP 8 7 6 5 4 3 2 1 0 9

Printed and bound in Canada

INDEX

Yukon

Alaska highway, 12, 14, 20, 21
Artists, 29
Aviation, 15

Bell, John, 7
Bering, Vitus, 7
Berton, Pierre, 28

Campbell, Robert, 7
Caribou, 5, 14, 30, 31
Carmack, George, 8
Climate, 5
Communities, 20, 21

Dawson City, 10-11, 13, 18, 21, 29
Dempster highway, 14, 15
Dene, 3
Discovery Day, 26, 27

Education, 24
Entertainment, 29
Eskimos, see Inuit
Explorers, 7

Farming, 19
Faro, 16, 21, 29
Festivals, 26-7
Fishing, 19
Forests, 5, 18-19
Franklin, Sir John, 7

Glaciers, 4, 30, 31
Gold rush, 8-11, 18
Government, 22-23

Harrison, Ted, 29
Health care, 25
Hudson's Bay Company, 7
Hydroelectric power, 19

Indian rights, 26, 30
Inuit, 3, 6

Kabloona, 3
Klondike highway, 14
Kluane National Park, 4, 18, 30

Lakes, 4, 19
London, Jack, 28

Minerals, 4, 13
Mining, 16-17. *See also* Gold rush
Mountains, 4, 30
Mounted police, 10, 11

Old Crow, 20, 21

Parks, 4, 18, 30
Pipelines, 12, 15, 26

Railroads, 15
Riverboats, 12-13, 21
Rivers, 5, 19, 31
Roads, 12, 14, 15

Robb, Jim, 29
Service, Robert, 3, 28
Sourdough Rendezvous, 26, 27

Tourism, 18, 20, 21, 27, 29, 30
Transportation, 14-15
Trapping, 19

Walsh, James, 11
Watson Lake, 20, 21
Whitehorse, 15, 18, 21, 22, 23, 24, 25, 26, 29
Wilderness areas, 30-31
Wildlife, 30, 31
Writers, 28

Northwest Territories

Administration, 52,3
Arctic circle, 33
Arctic Winter Games, 60
Arnaktauyok, Germaine, 59
Arts and crafts, 58-9
Auyuittuq National Park, 34, 47
Aviation, 48, 50

Baffin, William, 38
Baffin Island, 38
Berger Commission, 45

Cardinal, Don, 59
Caribou, 33, 34, 35, 46
Climate, 33
Communities, 54-5

Davis, John, 38
Dempster highway, 49
Dene, 36, and throughout
Dogs, 49

Eskimos, see Inuit
Explorers, 38, 39, 40, 41

Festivals, 61
Fishing, 46, 47
Forest, 33
Fort Resolution, 43
Fort Smith, 54
Franklin, Sir John, 40, 41
Frobisher, Martin, 38, 44
Frobisher Bay, 42, 55
Fur trade, 39, 43, 54

Geology, 32
Gold, 42, 44

Hay River, 54
Health care, 56
Hearne, Samuel, 39, 44
Houston, James, 58, 59
Hudson, Henry, 38
Hudson's Bay Company, 39, 42, 43, 51

Igloos, 51
Inuit, 37, and throughout
Inukshuit, 62
Inuktitut, 53
Inuvik, 54, 55

Judiciary, 53

Kabloonas, 42, 43, 46, 51

Lakes, 33
Languages, 53

McClintock, Capt. Francis, 41
Mackenzie, Alexander, 39, 44
Mackenzie highway, 49, 54
Mackenzie river, 39, 40, 44, 49
Mining, 44-5
Mouchet, Father Jean-Marie, 60-61
Mountains, 32
Musk oxen, 35, 46

Nahanni National Park, 34, 47
Natural gas, 45
Norman Wells, 42, 44, 45, 54
North West Company, 39
North-west passage, 38, 39, 40, 41

Oil, 42, 44
Outpost program, 51

Parks, 34, 47
Parry, Capt. William, 40
Pine Point, 45, 54
Pingos, 34
Pipeline, 45
Population, 54

Rae, Dr. John, 41
Richardson, John, 40, 41
Rivers, 33
Roads, 48-9
Ross, Capt. James, 41
Royal Canadian Mounted Police, 42

Schools, 57
Sissons, Jack, 43
Snowmobiles, 49, 51
Sports, 60-61

Territorial council, 52
Tourism, 47
Transportation, 48-9
Trapping, 46-7
Treeline, 33
Tundra, 33

Uranium, 42, 44

Virginia Falls, 34

Whaling industry, 43, 47
Wildlife, 34, 35, 46
Wood Buffalo National Park, 34, 47

Yellowknife, 42, 43, 49, 52, 54

CANADIAN STATISTICS

	Joined Confed- eration	Capital	Area	Population (1976)	Ethnic Origin (% 1971)		
					British	French	Other
CANADA		Ottawa	9 976 185 km²	22 992 604	45	29	26
Newfoundland	1949	St. John's	404 519 km²	557 725	94	3	3
Prince Edward Island	1873	Charlottetown	5 657 km²	118 229	83	14	3
Nova Scotia	1867	Halifax	55 491 km²	828 571	77	10	13
New Brunswick	1867	Fredericton	74 437 km²	677 250	58	37	5
Quebec	1867	Quebec City	1 540 687 km²	6 234 445	11	79	10
Ontario	1867	Toronto	1 068 587 km²	8 264 465	59	10	31
Manitoba	1870	Winnipeg	650 090 km²	1 021 506	42	9	49
Saskatchewan	1905	Regina	651 903 km²	921 323	42	6	52
Alberta	1905	Edmonton	661 188 km²	1 838 037	47	6	47
British Columbia	1871	Victoria	948 600 km²	2 466 608	58	4	38
Yukon	—	Whitehorse	536 327 km²	21 836	49	7	56
Northwest Territories	—	Yellowknife	3 379 699 km²	42 609	25	7	68